THE TRANSITION PLAYBOOK

Finding Purpose in Retirement as an Athlete

BY

STUART MCCONNELL

kp

ISBN: 978-1-990728-27-3 (Hardcover)
ISBN: 978-1-990728-26-6 (Paperback)
ISBN: 978-1-990728-41-9 (Ebook)

DEDICATION

This book is dedicated to all the incredible athletes out there who go beyond what us mere mortals do on a daily basis. I deeply believe that when the time comes to leave sports and you choose to point all that drive and passion in a new direction to make a difference on this planet, you will be the game changers. It's in your DNA.

TABLE OF CONTENTS

YOUR PLAYBOOK FOR RETIREMENT CHALLENGES AS AN ATHLETE

You've always known that at some point you would no longer be able to compete, but you've never turned your attention to what would be next. When you think about it: you've worked your ass off most of your life to get from A to B and now you realize that you have no idea what C is. In fact, a 2009 study found that within two years of their careers ending seventy-eight percent of NFL retirees have "gone bankrupt or are under financial stress because of joblessness or divorce" and "within five years of retirement, an estimated sixty percent of former NBA players are broke." It's scary and unnerving moving into the unknown territory of life after sports.

Now retirement is upon you and it's time to deal with it. And a lot of uncertainty pops up:

- What do I do next?
- What's my purpose now?

- Who am I outside of being a pro athlete?
- How do I fill the void left by not competing anymore?

"I knew what it took to be an Olympic Athlete but how the #%@& do I become successful as an entrepreneur?!? How do I translate what it takes to be the best in the world in sport into business?" – Martha Henderson (Olympic Sailor)

In my research, I have found that there are ten notable areas and challenges that affect an athlete entering this transitionary period. All must be addressed in order to move through this phase with velocity and power to create the next version of you – someone who celebrates love, joy, connection, gratitude and purpose every day of their lives.

Research has shown that it typically takes four to eight years to adjust to a new life.

Seventy-eight percent of NFL retirees have gone bankrupt or are under financial stress within two years of retirement.

This book was written to shed light on all the challenges high level athletes encounter in retirement and the opportunities that are available out of dealing with them. It is put together in a way to address all aspects of you – mind, body, and spirit. I have found the biggest missing piece is that no one, likely including yourself, is looking at your transition holistically. Many professionals help in one specialized area (i.e., career planning, financial planning, or psychology) but typically, no one takes a 'whole person' approach. There are more challenges that you, a retiring athlete, face than just finding a job that you like. All aspects of your life are interconnected.

MIND

1. New career path (who will hire me – unsure of transferrable skills)

2. Unhealthy connection to, or, complete disconnect from your sport post retirement

3. Blame and dwelling on the past

4. Lack of structure post retirement

BODY

1. Change in physical demands – biochemical and nutritional changes

2. Addiction to your emotions

SPIRIT

1. Loss of identity

2. Loss of purpose

3. The void that is left (feeling of something missing)

4. Feeling incomplete with your sports career

PART I

MIND

*"Sports is a game, **life** is a **game**, business is a game. And, and as soon as you stop taking yourself too seriously and you recognize it for what it is, you can have some fun with it. You can turn it into whatever you want."*

- Christopher Cook (Olympic Sailor)

CHAPTER 1

FROM FIELD TO OFFICE: LEVERAGING YOUR TRANSFERRABLE SKILLS IN A NEW CAREER ARENA

CHALLENGE

You may have a degree or diploma from a college or university, but even with that education or training, many athletes are nervous about entering a new career. The internal conversation is usually something like this:

"I spent all my time focusing on being an athlete, I don't remember anything else I learned in school. All my skills are focused on my sport and athletics. What else am I good at?"

The fact is that you got so confident and comfortable doing something that you were exceptionally good at and now you're expected to do something where you feel you have no proficiency. It's an unnerving place to be.

You see the skills honed in your sport as only being useful to succeed in that space. But when you break down the skills that you developed over the years to get to the top of your game, you'll find an incredibly strong skill set that is highly transferrable.

The following may be a funny way to look at it, but it's an illustrative example. A successful drug dealer has a myriad of transferrable skills that are highly coveted by companies for middle management or even C-suite level positions:

1. Customer retention – how to give the customer what they want while keeping your costs down (and not killing them)
2. How to lower overhead through minimizing losses
3. A great leader – for their organization to be the most profitable they must know how to get people to do what they want them to do. The better they understand how to motivate their employees the more their business will grow.
4. Creative problem solving – things are always changing and happening, especially the more successful their organization becomes. Thinking on their feet to solve problems saves money.

Like I said – an odd example but it drives the point home. If a drug dealer has all those transferrable skills imagine how many you have!

Alan Spector, a retirement planning consultant, and author said: "Elite athletes have developed skills and experience that have made them successful in their profession, and they're the exact same skills that you need to be successful in retirement. Understanding the game you're gonna be playing, assessing strengths and weaknesses, recognizing circumstances as they change and adjusting your game plan ... that's the same thing an athlete does at a game."

OPPORTUNITY

This is a great opportunity to have a look back over your career and what it took from you to achieve the level of success you have. Once you have identified your best skills then begin to use them in a very deliberate way to help you get what you want in life.

LIFE BEYOND THE ICE: SCOTT'S JOURNEY OF REDISCOVERING PURPOSE AFTER COMPETITIVE SKATING

I got started as a professional skater through my good friend Karen Preston. She had gone down to the U.S. to be Snow White in the Disney on Ice show. One of the high-profile male skaters tore his ACL, I think. It was something horrible. And he was out for the rest of the show. Karen phoned me up and said, "This guy just dropped, like on the ice yesterday and we need a guy – you could do it – would you do it?"

I didn't really take it very seriously, but I said, "Sure I'll talk to them about it."

So, the booker for Disney phoned about ten minutes later and said, "Karen filled us in on everything about you. Are you comfortable traveling around the world? You got a passport? You know, all this stuff?" and I was like, yes, yes, yes, yes. She said, "All right we're sending you a plane ticket. You're leaving in the morning."

Ten o'clock in the morning I was out and I was in Knoxville, Tennessee by about six o'clock in the afternoon skating for Disney on Ice. Physically, figure skating is a wonderful feeling. There's a lot of sensations, it's great; nothing quite like it. It's really like you get a little hit of a drug.

Eventually, I got to a point where I was tired of living out of suitcases. It's a great job, but you're stripped of everything. You have to take it all with you and it can only weigh "X" amount. That's it. So I had two seventy pound bags and my skates. That was my whole life. It was wanting more of the little luxury things that made me want to get off the road. When I retired from Olympic skating, I was twenty-eight years old. I think when I got off the road with Disney, I was very close to thirty. I took my skates off, flew home and then I never put my skates on for about fifteen years? – until last year, and that was for my son.

When I came back, I really didn't know what to do. I only had a high school education. I had taken some college and university level prep courses and I thought about going into kinesiology. I'm a smart guy. I could have done that. But then I also thought what about traveling the world, when are you going to do that? I had no idea what to do with myself at all.

Music wasn't even what I was thinking of getting into immediately, because I needed to make money somehow. I was fine for the short-term, but I certainly wasn't a billionaire. I couldn't just quit my job and do nothing. I had to do something. So, I had to figure out – what am I going to learn? What am I going to do? If I had to do it for eight hours a day? And working for Disney was three hours a day? What would I be okay, doing for five more hours a day? At Disney we had twenty-two hours a day off. Like you only went to work to do that show, which was two hours long and when it was over, you're on your own recognizance. Good luck. See you tomorrow. Thank you. You know, that's it. So that was life, you were just on free time. Needless to say, it was a challenge trying to fit into a corporate environment.

I tested my hand at a few different work things that were okay. I like electronics and have kind of an aptitude for it. My father is sort of invested in those types of fields and got me into doing a little bit of contracting with him for installing CCTV, access control and things like that. So, I did that with him for a couple of years and then we bid on higher and higher contracts because I liked to read the manuals for all the boards, like how to program it, and then I would figure that puzzle out. We were pretty good together and it was a lot of fun.

What I've learned is that having a degree doesn't guarantee you happiness in work. I would tell others to really spend a lot of time before you get too invested [in sports] trying to find out what your other major interests are. Everybody has something. Know what that is, while you work on your sport. And then figure out how to prepare for doing that when you retire. Because you want to be happy when sports are over.

For almost thirty years every time I turned around there were people hounding at me to get me to do things to try to bring me here or, can you be on this team? Can you do this? Because a boy in figure skates was rare. Even in the professional world, a lot of our shows would be fifty-five women and seven men on a tour. It wasn't celebrity but I never had to look for work or anything. It was always beating down my door. Going into the 'normal working world' suddenly all of your skill set, all of your everything that you are really special at, well that's not what employers are looking for. So, I think having that period where you realize that you're not special anymore, and not knowing what direction to go, what to do or how do you fix it was very important. I think everything that you're doing, especially if you're flailing, is important. Everything easy right now is likely not going to be what you need.

You gotta keep on plugging, and just remember, whatever the transition is, people hate change. The best way to get through change is just remember that the process of change is temporary. So, when you're in those positions, don't get bogged down on how bad today was.

For me it reminds me of training. I didn't like leg day. It happened multiple times a week and it was awful. I knew it would be bad going in and it was bad after I was done. I never liked it. It sucked. But I did it. Because I was moving towards something. You have to keep that in mind. Because it's hard when you don't have a clear goal like when you were an athlete; but remember that there still is a goal. You just haven't seen it yet.

OPPORTUNITY (REMINDER)

This is a great opportunity to have a look back over your career and what it took from you to achieve the level of success you have. Once you have identified your best skills then begin to use them in a very deliberate way to help you get what you want in life.

CHAPTER 2

FINDING BALANCE AFTER RETIREMENT: HEALTHY TIES AND NECESSARY BREAKS FROM SPORTS

CHALLENGE

Unhealthy Connection:

An unhealthy connection happens when someone is obsessed with either getting back into competition, pushing others to compete at high levels (in an emotionally unhealthy way for the participant), or continually hanging around the team they once competed for. These are all about one thing – trying to remain connected to what meant so much to them for so long.

Complete Disconnection:

This occurs for one of two reasons:

1. Either the belief that the pain of being connected to your sport in any way would be too great to handle, or

2. When you were competing, you weren't happy or fulfilled and the experience left a 'bad taste in your mouth'. For many, this is the case if you were pushed to compete (e.g., parents) when you didn't want to and/or you pursued your sport only to please other people and not for your own joy and fulfillment.

OPPORTUNITY

The opportunity here is to create a healthy connection where you keep your sport or athletics in general in your life in a way that not only adds to it, but also to the lives of others. You dedicated so much of your life to being an athlete at the highest level. In your heart, you are an athlete: you always will be in one way or another. To not pass on your love of athleticism and your hard-earned wisdom would be doing the world a disservice. Looking at it from the perspective of "What can I do to give back to the sport that gave me so much?" is a very empowering context that can ripple through all aspects of your life.

Even if you are happy to be moving on, there are opportunities to help others (e.g., young kids) who are struggling with the same issues and pressures you did, who can use guidance and support.

If you don't want to be involved in sports in any way, consider how effective you could be in motivating others to push past their physical and mental limits, enabling them to accomplish their goals in business or life. Through this you are still connecting to the part of your heart that is the athlete.

BEYOND THE GRIDIRON:
HOW RAY FOUND SUCCESS ON AND OFF THE FIELD

While I was a playing professional football, I knew the longevity of that career was limited. I was fortunate to be able to find a parallel career opportunity and took advantage of my time outside of the football season and began a full-time job as an account manager for a staffing agency. It was important for me to build the foundation for a career outside football when the time came, and I was able to work for a company that saw the value of hiring a CFL player and allowing the flexibility to continue my athletic career while also working full-time in the corporate world.

On one hand there were a few players like me who were blending a professional football career while working in the corporate world. On the other hand, there were many more teammates who were not. The challenge for them was that they may have been playing for years and by the time they were finished with football due to being cut, retirement, or injury, they might be about 35 years old and going into the workforce without any practical work experience. I said to myself: I do not want to be that guy.

But it is different for each individual. Some guys do that [not work at other jobs] and they are successful. But what I found is that if you can set yourself up for an easier transition then why wouldn't you?

I probably would have played longer had I not won a Grey Cup. The fact that I won one, it kind of capped off my career. I may have been able to push myself to play another two, maybe three years. But I started to think realistically about a few things like my age, the toll my body was taking, etc. Another key factor was that I had not had any major injuries, no surgeries and being a football player, that was a blessing. I had also just become a dad and that played a factor as well.

So, I get to the point that I start thinking, okay, I have had eight great years, do I want to play nine? In the back of my mind, I'm thinking "You're going to play your ninth and blow out your knee or something." It was at that time that I said, I would rather leave on my terms than go through training camp again. It is a head game.

I had seen players who played for thirteen years, they want to push for one more, they go to camp give it their all, and are cut, that's it, you're done, game over. I had witnessed how traumatic it can be for veterans to experience that rejection, that loss of control over their career. And, although I did end on my own terms, it was still hard mentally and impacted my identity as a person. I remember the first year it was tough to even go to the games, to not be a part of the team. I felt like I did not want to be seen. I think I only went to one or two games that year. I just stayed away from it because it was like my identity was tied to football and now it was over. I was not sure how to handle it.

Those first few years were mentally challenging, I tried to make it look like it leaving the game had not really impacted me. After all, leaving was my decision. What I really missed was not the camps or practices, it was the feeling that came with game day. The adrenaline rush of coming out of the tunnel and running onto the field with your team, in front of the cheering fans, giving them everything you had both physically and mentally, there was no other feeling like it. I missed that high level of competition and the comradery with my teammates. It was hard to recreate that feeling off the field in the corporate world – it was not the same adrenaline rush. In retirement I was not necessarily trying to replace that feeling but it is challenging to re-create that exhilaration that you had become accustomed to physically and mentally.

My first year after leaving the CFL, I was promoted to manager and took over one of the divisions at the company I worked for. My responsibilities had increased, and I was starting to feel challenged again and was starting to accept the reality of my football career being over. But I must admit, that even after that first year of not playing, and not going to the games I would watch the sports channel and catch a few plays and think, "I could still do that, I know I can" or "I'm faster than he is". It took me a few years to really say I am done with this and not consider trying to go back.

Looking back now, I did not realize how leaving the game impacted my mental health. I stayed away from getting involved with football for a long time after retirement. But it's funny how things happen. Football once again became a major part of my life when I got into coaching. It happened that one of the gentlemen who started the Calgary Minor Football Association, reached out to me about possibly coaching. I told him I was not interested. He was persistent and said to me 'One of these years I'm gonna get you coaching." So, every year, I'd see him and every year he'd ask again and again.

It was at this point that my son was about Six or seven and was playing baseball, soccer, and hockey, but he started to ask me about trying out for football. When he started playing atom football, I got the dreaded question and this time, I relented. So began my youth minor football coaching career. I remember seeing my old friend and the first thing he says is, "See I told you I'd get you coaching." And it was one of the best decisions I have made.

I was able to help coach my son all the way up into high school. I helped his high school team, and now I have continued coaching. I have also been able to enjoy the game from the stands – my greatest moment as a football fan was watching my son win the 2019 Vanier Cup National Football Championship.

Coaching football has been one of my most fulfilling life endeavors, to be able to give back to a sport that had given me so much. It is genuinely great to be able to mentor young players and help them to achieve their goals on and off the field.

For me, my identify with football came full circle. While it is not the major focus of my life that it once was many years ago – it has its place. My true focus is on my faith, my family, and my career – but coaching has brought me the opportunity to get back on that field and share that adrenaline rush with the great kids I have the privilege to teach the game.

I chose to still be tied to the sport that I love through coaching the younger generation – but it took a long while to get there. I can coach these young men and I am able to have an impact on their lives. I have become a mentor to many players, and I see that as a true honour. I stay connected with other coaches and principals in Calgary so I can keep tabs on players that might be struggling on or off the field. I can talk to players about choices they make, etc. It is sometimes a bit different coming from their coach than when mom and dad have that conversation with them.

Once you start to get older in pro sports your love of the game can dwindle because you start to see more of the politics and the business side of the game. I remember telling myself that if I ever got to a point where I do not like the game anymore then it was time to quit. I never got to that point, thankfully. But I always remember how much I loved playing the game.

OPPORTUNITY (REMINDER)

The opportunity here is to create a healthy connection where you keep your sport or athletics in general in your life in a way that not only adds to it, but also to the lives of others. You dedicated so much of your life to being an athlete at the highest level. In your heart, you are an athlete: you always will be in one way or another. To not pass on your love of athleticism and your hard-earned wisdom would be doing the world a disservice. Looking at it from the perspective of "What can I do to give back to the sport that gave me so much?" is a very empowering context that can ripple through all aspects of your life.

Even if you are happy to be moving on, there are opportunities to help others (e.g., young kids) who are struggling with the same issues and pressures you did, who can use guidance and support.

If you don't want to be involved in sports in any way, consider how effective you could be in motivating others to push past their physical and mental limits, enabling them to accomplish their goals in business or life. Through this you are still connecting to the part of your heart that is the athlete.

CHAPTER 3

BREAKING FREE FROM THE CYCLE OF BLAME AND REGRET: CREATING A FUTURE WITH A LOT LESS BAGGAGE

CHALLENGE

You've competed for the last time and your career as an athlete is officially over. The reality of the situation suddenly hits you – there is no practice tomorrow, or ever again, and you have no idea what you're going to do moving forward. This is when the should-haves, regret, and blame start running the show. "Why was I not prepared for this?" You've mapped out every other aspect of your career thus far, until now.

It's typical to blame yourself or others when things in your life aren't going the way you want them to. It's easy to get caught up in that cycle of blame and shame and use it as an excuse to not move forward. When you sit in blame all you're doing is spending your valuable time and energy focusing on something from the past that you can't change. Nothing gets resolved and you're certainly not focusing on what there is for you to do now to move yourself forward. When you were competing, you would have learned and moved on, you would not have wasted energy in this way.

The more you focus on the past the less you can see your present or future. It can become all-consuming and keeps you stuck in one place as your mind replays thoughts, events, or conversations over and over like they are on a loop.

First baseman Aubrey Huff has said about his battle with depression post-retirement: *"What am I going to be now that my baseball career is over, I'm a professional baseball player but now I'm not. I was depressed because I was thinking about the past."*

It can become emotionally unhealthy if you're not aware of what is going on. The key is to keep yourself in the present moment as much as you can. It is the most efficient way to have the life you want as soon as you want.

Chances are you don't even notice how much energy you're dedicating to these thoughts. Whether it's over your lack of planning, or what you should have, or could have done differently – if you look closely, it's there. We all do it. Because beating ourselves up or blaming others is much easier than taking responsibility by owning where you're at without judgement.

OPPORTUNITY

First off, stop beating yourself up over what you or someone else did (or didn't) do. Of course, getting over things from your past is, in many instances, easier said than done. The past is gone and cannot be changed. This running dialogue that you don't even notice is taking up valuable resources and colouring your perception of the life that you're creating moving forward. Focus on the present and consider that every day is a new opportunity to create the life that you want.

Lastly, take 100% responsibility for where you are and how you got there. This is the most powerful thing you can do for yourself because it is only from this context that you have the ability to change your life. If you got yourself to where you are, you can get yourself somewhere else. When you put the blame on others you make them responsible and cede all power over the situation. The opportunity here is to create a new context for your life moving forward. Take the time to deliberately examine and create the next chapter in your life not based on could-haves or should-haves. You may feel like you've started it already and may not be happy with the direction it has taken but the good news is that you can turn another page and start another chapter.

BOUNCING BACK: HOW JAN-MICHAEL TURNED ADVERSITY INTO SELF-DISCOVERY AND RESILIENCE

I was playing for a team in the north of England when I got injured trying out for a team in France. Instead of going back home, my friend (Phil) said, Listen, come with me, stay with me in Liverpool, help me start up my own basketball team, and basketball academy. I'll pay for the rehab on your ankle and we'll go from there. Phil was a great guy who helped me get started playing in England. I even stayed with him for a time when I first got there.

So, I helped him set up his team and Academy. We had to start off in the lower divisions so to help raise money. I did a lot of basketball camps and helped him write proposals to the government for funding and so forth. I coached teams and played for the men's team. We won our divisions twice and got promoted up. In the third year, things are going according to the plan, we're getting more money, we're getting more exposure, we were winning, and things were going well. But as it turns out, my friend was running the club into debt. Even though we were undefeated during the season we weren't getting our pay on time.

When I came back in September of that year, I got my first month's pay, I got my second month's pay, and the third month, I got half of it. Phil, by this time, is like an older brother to me, I love this guy, I put my trust in his hands believing what he was telling me; "The money is coming they're just holding it because you're an international player". The fourth month came, we got no money. And now guys are getting a little bit more frustrated. Some of the guys had children, they had to send money to their families, and they were starting to feel the pinch. We weren't getting money and Phil wasn't being honest. Right before the Christmas break, the team executives held a private meeting with us import players and the shareholders of the club. They notified us that Phil had run the club into over 50,000 pounds worth of debt.

They were so far behind in debts that they don't know if they could pay us our full salary for the remainder of the year. This was a huge wake up call. This was a close friend, he helped me start my opportunity, and here I am finding out that he's been cheating us out of our own money. So, they gave him and his wife an ultimatum. They both were forced to resign, and we continued on for the season. My goal was to spite him, try to win and then get as much money as I could out of the club before going home. Unfortunately for us, we ended up losing in a championship game, and got blown out. I stayed about a month and a half after, and I tried to collect as much money as I could from what they owed me. But at that point my love for the game was just kind of stripped away from me. This was such a disheartening situation because I LOVE basketball, it saved my life. And to have the love kind of stripped away from me, kind of killed it, it hurt me inside.

Coming back home, things went from bad to worse. It was a struggle and a reality check. You know, before I was playing games and having fans come at me and cheer me and put me on a pedestal, and back home, no one knows of my accomplishments. It was a huge ego shattering moment. I had a relationship here and I found out that person wasn't being faithful so that was kind of a shot to the heart. When I first came back, I had money that I was going to exchange into Canadian dollars. I was taking my grandmother to the hospital, to get her eyes checked out and someone broke into my car and they stole all the money, all my stuff. So, all the money that I made from that last year was gone. That was a very heartbreaking moment. It was just a series of events that spiraled me into a depression. What I did, which was the worst thing I could have done at that time, was I isolated myself away from those who I trusted and loved. I didn't see anyone for like a year. I was kind of ashamed of myself at that time because I didn't have a clear understanding what was going on and I was just kind of forced into a new perspective of life. I was trying to pick up the pieces, but I just didn't feel I had a strong foundation underneath me.

I was there in that depression for pretty much the majority of a year and then I got a phone call from my mom. And I'll never forget it. She gave me an inspiring call, basically saying get up off my ass, and start moving, pull my head out of my ass basically, to start moving and get things going. Even though it wasn't something I wanted to hear, it's something I needed to hear, and I love her for it. It got the ball rolling. What I started doing was start feeling good about myself physically. I started working out at home, doing little things to kind of boost my self-esteem. Then I started looking for work. It was all a gradual process. I started socializing again, started talking, like even talking about it now so many years removed from it, but it was very therapeutic at the time.

I definitely appreciate the experiences that I went through because it helped shape me into the person I am. I appreciate where I am now because I have those experiences to kind of base my decisions going forward. I can help mentor other people and I have a strong relationship with my friends and family. I became a man in England, you know, I started to figure out who I was, and my place within the world. And then when I came back, I stumbled, but I was able to pick up the pieces and start moving forward again. I have a new sense of Self, I understand my place in the world, and my influences on the people around me.

I was glad to go through the situation of playing ball from when I was 23 and finishing when I was 33. When one chapter closes, another one begins. It's like a continuous journey. We're all on our individual journeys. And the great thing about it is, we are in control of what happens next.

OPPORTUNITY (REMINDER)

First off, stop beating yourself up over what you or someone else did (or didn't) do. Of course, getting over things from your past is, in many instances, easier said than done. The past is gone and cannot be changed. This running dialogue that you don't even notice is taking up valuable resources and colouring your perception of the life that you're creating moving forward. Focus on the present and consider that every day is a new opportunity to create the life that you want.

Lastly, take 100% responsibility for where you are and how you got there. This is the most powerful thing you can do for yourself because it is only from this context that you have the ability to change your life. If you got yourself to where you are, you can get yourself somewhere else. When you put the blame on others you make them responsible and cede all power over the situation. The opportunity here is to create a new context for your life moving forward. Take the time to deliberately examine and create the next chapter in your life not based on could-haves or should-haves. You may feel like you've started it already and may not be happy with the direction it has taken but the good news is that you can turn another page and start another chapter.

CHAPTER 4

REINVENTING YOUR DAILY BLUEPRINT: BUILDING PURPOSEFUL ROUTINES

CHALLENGE

It's likely that you have followed very specific routines for many years now. These routines bring order and structure to your life and have become habitual. They take some of the guess work out of life and enable you to focus the maximum amount of your energy where it is needed most – on improving your performance.

In retirement, the need for your old routines and structures is gone. When the structure is gone, the ability to focus, plan, prioritize, and get things done can become difficult and overwhelming. It's like you were on autopilot that has been switched off and you now have to fly the plane by yourself, without a compass. It is easy to fall into making every day a 'vacation' day, unfettered and unrestrained – able to do whatever you want, whenever you want. However, that can only last for as long as you have money to it.

Trent Green former NFL quarterback had this to say about it: *"The hardest part is your daily routine. For fifteen years, I knew exactly what I was doing in March, June and September because there was a schedule. When you take that away, you suddenly have a lot more time on your hands. I've been out of the game since 2008, and I still have a tough time with it".*

To see the benefit of structure in real time try this exercise:

1. Take out two sheets of paper and a timer. Start the timer. On the first sheet draw a square in the middle of the page. Once you've completed it, fold the sheet in half and put it on the floor beside you. Stop the timer.

Reset your timer and start it. On the other sheet of paper draw whatever you like and do whatever you want with it, but you must do something with it. Stop the timer.

You may have noticed that it takes significantly more time to determine a direction in which to go when no parameters are given because the choices are seemingly endless. As well, it's easier to get lost in your own thoughts or change your mind five times if you haven't clearly defined your goal or purpose.

If you've been retired for a while and have spent much of your now-free time on your couch with your new best friend Netflix: you know this challenge all too well.

OPPORTUNITY

The opportunity here is to create a new set of routines for yourself that will help you have this next chapter be as good as, or better than, your last. Take the time to critically examine, and deliberately create structures from this context. This can greatly cut down on wasted time and needless drama and can add power and velocity to your life because what you create will be focused on what lights you up and pulls you forward.

Creating routines, habits, and structures is what many people overlook to have their lives work better.

CHARTING A NEW COURSE:
CHRIS' LESSONS FROM NAVIGATING THROUGH A SEA OF CHANGE

I transitioned out of competitive sailing, just because I felt like maybe "I'd caught that fish."

I remember exactly when it happened: it was actually right after the 2008 Olympics and then the 2009 sort of spring season. I was at a regatta in Europe, not really caring too much at this point, when I tacked on some guy and basically, I took his wind. But I was in front of him so it's my right to do it. He started spewing at me, in like a kind of Estonian/English hybrid of insults. I think I was fifth or sixth in the race and I looked back, and I thought, *What? I don't need this shit. What am I doing?* I just peeled off and sailed in. I took my boat apart, put it on the trailer, went back and cooked up some hamburgers. I got on a plane the next day and just left mid-regatta. I got home and I said to my wife, I'm done. That's it.

I stopped mid-year. That turned off my entire income. There was podium money, government, sponsorships etc. There were quite a few dollars that I turned off. I could have kept all of that stuff going but I realized that if I don't, then I'll never really be free of this. I wasn't not going to get anywhere if I had one foot in each thing. If I'm accepting money to do a job, then I need to do that job. And I'm not prepared to do it.

I decided I was going to be a real estate agent and try something completely new. Right when I started the courses, I got a job offer to coach. I didn't have a clue how to sell houses, but I did know sailing, so it was more aligned with what I know how to do. Plus being on the water sounded like more fun than doing all these courses.

So, I did that for two years and I was working for somebody else, which I'd never really done before, and I hated it. My boss was my old training partner and a good friend, and I just couldn't do it anymore. For whatever reason, I thought it would be better if I worked instead for the national team. I thought if I was a national team coach, then I could be in charge. I made a deal with them that if I came back and sailed for another year that I could get this job. It was the worst reason to come back and do something. I was doing something that I was already finished with to get something else that I THOUGHT I wanted. So, I did it. I had some fun doing it, it was a great year, and I spent a lot of money.

At the end of the day, my heart wasn't in it, and I got sick, I was knocked right out. Normally if it was something that I really wanted; I would have just worked past it. But I just couldn't summon myself to do it. I thought to myself, *What am I doing? This is crazy. I'm almost forty. I'm still sailing, and this is crazy. What am I doing?* And so that's how it was basically the end of it. I didn't qualify for the Olympics, and I was happy about that because I didn't want to do another four or five months. I just wanted to go home.

I wanted to get on with my life and do my thing. That meant more coaching and more away time. I did that for two more years and then I just had this moment with my new boss where I was thinking *Why are you paying us if you're not going to listen to what we have to say? Are you a national team coach or are you an administrator—you're telling us how to create athletes? This is ridiculous.* So, I quit. Which was crazy because at that point we had a kid. But I just couldn't do it. I went and worked for my Danish buddy and coached him for eight months and got my real estate license, which I always intended on doing.

But it's amazing. What I found most frustrating was that I spent my whole life—up until that moment—believing in myself, overcoming challenges, and pushing through hard stuff. As soon as it came to actually creating my "real life," I was lost. All of a sudden, I had to get a job and work for somebody else. I had just accomplished all of these really, really big things and then I felt like I cut myself off at the legs – I couldn't figure out how to do something else on my own, that suits me and makes me happy. I found that really frustrating. That sort of realization that I just spent five years doing something that didn't match up with who I am and what I want to do with my life. That's why I can really sympathize with a lot of athletes that are coming up on the "finish line" of their careers.

People get stressed about what's happening with their peers while they're off doing the "sport thing," and that they're falling behind. What I found was as soon as I stopped trying to hold on to what was no longer a fit for me and started focusing on something different than I love (which happened to be real estate) I had surpassed all of those friends within a year. Also, as an athlete I'm way healthier and probably have more energy at forty-six than my counterparts did at thirty.

I really feel that athletes need to understand better, while they're competing, what it is they're creating in and for themselves. Nobody cares how high you can jump; not really. Not ten years, five years, a year after you're done being an athlete—truly nobody cares how high you can jump. They care what kind of person you've become as a result of what you did. What did that experience leave you with? When you're done being an athlete, draw on that experience and apply it to whatever comes next. You want to be a coach and that's your life dream? Great. Fantastic. Please do that. But if you don't, if you do want to leave sport, it doesn't matter what you touch, you're gonna be better than anybody else that didn't have that experience. I think it's because we understand the value of doing a little bit at a time to get to that top level while at the same time, being impatient, being hungry and wanting it faster.

OPPORTUNITY (REMINDER)

The opportunity here is to create a new set of routines for yourself that will help you have this next chapter be as good as, or better than, your last. Take the time to critically examine, and deliberately create structures from this context. This can greatly cut down on wasted time and needless drama and can add power and velocity to your life because what you create will be focused on what lights you up and pulls you forward.

Creating routines, habits, and structures is what many people overlook to have their lives work better.

PART II

BODY

"It's an adrenaline addiction. And when you lose your source of how to feed it, where are you going to get it again? Are you going to get it again?"

- Martha Henderson (Olympic Sailor)

CHAPTER 5

REDEFINING FITNESS AND DIET: NAVIGATING BIOCHEMICAL AND NUTRITIONAL CHANGES

CHALLENGE

The change in physical demands and exercise your body needs now that you're retired, like nutrition requirements, is also obvious but I believe its importance is greatly overlooked. You no longer need to train hard, for numerous hours every day, doing things that you might not enjoy that much (like burpees) – so what will you do to keep active? How will you stay accountable with no goals or reasons to push yourself?

Also, as you deal with many of the emotional stresses of retirement, it's easy to 'self-medicate' with food. Or you may want to take a diet vacation, binging on all of the foods you denied yourself over the years. It's also easy to keep eating like you were when you were training because your diet and food consumption have become habitual as well.

One challenge is to be feeding your body according to its needs now. Your body is accustomed to eating certain types of food, specific amounts of calories, and at certain times of day. When you initially change those factors, your body will give you indicators that you're not doing what is expected—like hunger, low energy etc. It is easy to misinterpret those signals to mean there is something wrong instead of it just being the adjustment period needed.

The second challenge is your body, right down to your cellular structure, has certain expectations around a particular level of activity. Your cells have an expectation of certain biochemical 'cocktails' being received based on repeated delivery over time. When you stop being active, or dramatically reduce your activity level, you can throw your body into a biochemical mess. Then the body must deal with the biochemical mess that is created, which can lead to weight gain, mental and physical illness.

OPPORTUNITY

The opportunity is to be good to your body—you hammered away at it for years now it's time to honour it.

1. Enjoy food on a different level now that you don't have to be as rigid in your diet. Something interesting to try is "mindful eating." Create a sustainable diet that you can be happy with for the long term. Tapering back your nutritional consumption should be done alongside tapering your activity level (see the next section). It takes time for your body to adjust so be patient with it.

   This is about being deliberate about making dietary changes and understanding that your body needs time to adjust to its new requirements. Just as you need time to settle into YOU 2.0 your body needs time to settle into BODY 2.0.

2. Taper your activity level back to something that is manageable and consistent with your goals for this next chapter in your life.

It's a perfect time to find physical activities that you love doing, and that can easily be worked into your daily or weekly routine. It's a great opportunity to try some of the sports or activities that you have wanted to try but couldn't because of your career. You also now get to enjoy your workouts simply because it's something you love to do, and not because you must do it to reach a goal—an interesting shift and challenge for goal-oriented people.

3. Another opportunity is to create a set of goals for yourself where you can get others involved in some way to make it more interesting and hold you accountable. It's a great way to help you focus while connecting others to something you love. Well thought out goals are a great tool to give you focus and move your life forward in a purposeful way.

KNOCKING OUT ADVERSITY: HOW BOXING BECAME A HEALING JOURNEY FOR MIRANDA

To be honest, boxing for me was never about violence. But it actually gave my assault, my hurt a voice for the first time. And I'll be honest, when people think of boxing they think of this violent sport and people hurt. Most people that come to boxing are victims of trauma or have had exposure to trauma and they come as a part of the healing process. There's something extremely freeing, specifically about being a woman and being in the ring and not having to be nice and not having to be caring and not having to worry about anybody but just surviving and I think that process is kind of what helped me heal and realize all the supportive people around me. In boxing, you have a team of people supporting you. But when it's time to fight, there's no time out, or I'm tired or oh let's have a play. You have to survive for two minutes on your own. I think that really helped change my perspective on being able to overcome challenges.

For me, my challenge came from overtraining. I was in a very male dominated environment, and I had a disk in my back blow up. And when it first blew up, I kept training because I didn't want to say, "oh my back hurts". I was still very new, I only had two fights. But that led to emergency room surgery. I was injured for about eight months. You know, to be honest, it was quite challenging because I was an athlete my whole life and then I couldn't carry my own groceries. I was on nerve blockers, I was getting cortisone shots, the process was just extremely hard. And then the disc blew up. I went to the emergency room and had surgery that same day.

Believe it or not, I told them I needed to see my surgeon. I needed to see the guy who's gonna cut into my back. When he came, I told him "I'm going to quit my job as a mortgage broker, and I'm going to devote my life to the sport of boxing, but you have to make sure I can walk. I need to be able to walk in order to do that." Luckily, he did fix me, and I did quit my job as a mortgage broker, and I've been working in boxing ever since.

In 2010 I founded the Mentoring Juniors Kids Organization (MJKO). My dream was to create community champions through sport (specifically non-contact boxing). We focus on the needs of the whole person, teaching the fundamental benefits of social skills development, healthy food choices, mindfulness, belonging and physical activity through daily, free access to non-contact boxing.

Now ten years in, I've had over ten thousand young people come in and out of my boxing business, I'm involved with Boxing Jamaica, and I've even trained the prime minister. Many of the young people have lost their mom and dad, many have dealt with abuse, many of them have gone through a lot. Those kids have become my family. Seeing those kids go on to university or college or creating a family—those are the important things. That's what sport is right? Sport is about creating good humans and paying it forward. I think all the resistance that we have, even with retirement, is understanding. Yes, you went into sport to get an Olympic medal. But it's so much bigger than that, right? The Olympic medal is being a good human and helping people when they need help and understanding you're going to fall down, and you have to get back up. That should be why we're really in sport.

I think that for me as a coach, and as a person involved in hopefully creating a different system, at least for the athletes that I coach, is that you can have both. You can be an elite athlete and you can still love your sport and you can retire, and you can be okay. With all the politics and the money, and the hopes and the pressures, we forget that sports unite us and creates this amazing unstoppable person. It's like the little engine that could. That's why we do it. But it gets so lost. Once you find it again, watch out! Like me – I have no doubt that I will eventually have an athlete that goes to the Olympics, will I get to go with them? I don't know, because I'm not in control of that. But my athletes, they know who I am. I'm the person who takes them to the doctor's appointment, who gets them the stuff that they need, who's there when they win, who's there when they lose. It's why I love sports so much. I'm okay now with whatever my piece is. Because the people that matter most to me are my athletes, and they understand I will always have their back, you know, no matter what I like, I'll have their back. My coach always says, "you know, Miranda, what you've accomplished, outside of the ring is bigger than any Olympic medal you could have ever got."

The funny thing is, I'm still in touch with my surgeon now, and he said to me "you know, Miranda, you have taught me so much because I had no idea what the sport of boxing meant to you. You taught me to slow down and to appreciate the fact that for some people their sport, it's so big to them."

OPPORTUNITY (REMINDER)

The opportunity is to be good to your body—you hammered away at it for years now it's time to honour it.

4. Enjoy food on a different level now that you don't have to be as rigid in your diet. Something interesting to try is "mindful eating." Create a sustainable diet that you can be happy with for the long term. Tapering back your nutritional consumption should be done alongside tapering your activity level (see the next section). It takes time for your body to adjust so be patient with it.

    This is about being deliberate about making dietary changes and understanding that your body needs time to adjust to its new requirements. Just as you need time to settle into YOU 2.0 your body needs time to settle into BODY 2.0.

5. Taper your activity level back to something that is manageable and consistent with your goals for this next chapter in your life. It's a perfect time to find physical activities that you love doing, and that can easily be worked into your daily or weekly routine. It's a great opportunity to try some of the sports or activities that you have wanted to try but couldn't because of your career. You also now get to enjoy your workouts simply because it's something you love to do, and not because you must do it to reach a goal—an interesting shift and challenge for goal-oriented people.

6. Another opportunity is to create a set of goals for yourself where you can get others involved in some way to make it more interesting and hold you accountable. It's a great way to help you focus while connecting others to something you love. Well thought out goals are a great tool to give you focus and move your life forward in a purposeful way.

CHAPTER 6

REWIRING YOUR EMOTIONAL BLUEPRINT: UNDERSTANDING YOUR BODY'S ADDICTION TO EMOTIONS

CHALLENGE

We all have a chemical addiction. It's not to alcohol or pharmaceuticals it's to our emotions. You actually have a physical addiction to your emotions. Here's why (spoiler alert: I'm going to nerd out on biology here:

Neuropeptides are produced by neurons throughout the brain. Neuropeptides act as chemical messengers to cells throughout the body regulated through feedback loops indicating a particular physiological need (i.e., for water), or emotional response (i.e., anger). Essentially a function of neuropeptides is to manufacture the chemical 'recipes' that match our emotional experiences throughout our day.

Let's say you are in a situation that you connect to sadness. Your brain makes the recipe associated with our understandings of what sadness should feel like the brain releases that recipe into the bloodstream. The more we *stimulate* our cells with the chemical equivalent of an emotion the more the cells grow to expect those chemicals. When this does not happen, the body provides feedback that a response is needed, and we then oblige with an appropriate response. Responses are your thoughts, actions, or decisions to do certain things. These responses become learned after time resulting in habituated behaviour.

For the most part this isn't a bad thing. It happens to all of us every day and its no big deal it's just a body process. But on the other hand, have you ever made a bad decision on something in the face of knowing it's a bad decision then sitting there in the aftermath wondering why you made such a bad decision? Yeah, that's the emotional addiction this is all eluding to. We create experiences in our lives, consciously or unconsciously, to give us the emotional hit we are needing at the request of our bodies.

When you were a professional athlete you would have really intense emotions during training or competing your body got to a point where it began to crave the biochemical cocktail known as winning, or competing, or fill in the blank. Now without its regular rush of chemical from those intense emotions your cells/ body don't know what to do to fill that receptor. Hence one major reason you have the feeling of something missing on a deep level. Your body is actually telling you that's the case. It's telling you that there is a void that needs to be filled—but not how to fill it, especially in a positive way. In turn you search to unconsciously fill the void with anything that takes away the pain or emptiness feeling. You find something new to be addicted to and many times it isn't something that is for the true betterment of your life, it's for the sake of filling a space. What you choose to feed your cells with can be broken into three categories.

1. Distraction—doing your best to avoid dealing with how you feel. It's not always drugs and alcohol, it's also diving deeply into something else that fills all your time.

2. Negative feelings—given all the things going on with you as a retired athlete it's easy to get overwhelmed with negative emotions like feeling of inadequate, feeling sorry for yourself, aggressive behaviour etc.

3. Positive feelings—this is what you want to feed your cells with. Filling that space inside with love (love of others, of life, of anything or everything), happiness, or joy are all things that we strive to feel daily anyway. When you boil it all down it's why we pursue the things we pursue. Why not step it up and make them our primary feelings instead of relegating them to further down the list.

OPPORTUNITY

Making the change is not an overnight thing but it doesn't have to be a long painful process either. Now that you understand what is going on you can be more conscious about your decisions moving forward to feed yourself in the way that will have you live the post-sports life you want.

The way to trigger your body to make the change is deliberately flooding your body a new emotion (yes—to get addicted to if you want to look at it that way). Spend time everyday focusing on feeling the way you want to primarily feel—love, joy, abundant etc. Focus on feeling it throughout your whole body. If you lose focus gently bring it back but don't move on to anything else in your day until you feel it everywhere even if it's just for a few seconds to start. It's a great practice to start and end your day with.

I know many of you will probably want to choose the same thing that was there: winning and being an awesome warrior (or some flavour of that). The problem is that the level of intensity you are used to feeling it at isn't possible on an everyday basis without being in competitive sport—which you aren't in anymore. To dial it down to a lower level isn't as easy as feeding your cells with something else.

Lastly, if after hearing all of that and making it this far into the book and you still making excuses that you can make it work then YOU ARE STUCK IN YOUR ADDICTION. It is your addiction talking, desiring more and willing to do anything to get it. Now is the time to apply your will and trust that your way forward is through choosing something new.

LIFE AT THE TOP TO STARTING OVER: MARTHA'S STORY OF REBUILDING HER IDENTITY POST-OLYMPICS

I remember getting off the plane after the Olympic Games in China. The plane was amazing, the ride home was awesome, it was the whole Canadian team and such great energy. Then the bottom fell out of it. We landed and everybody splintered off and I got home and that was it. It was over.

I got home at the end of August—which is significant because that is kind of the wind down of the sailing season here in Toronto—so there wasn't a lot to go back to. I had a lot of debt, and there was a lot of panic about where and how I was going to live. I was lucky that I was house-sitting for a friend and didn't have a lot of expenses. But my brain was constantly thinking, *oh my God, where do I start, how do I fix this?* It was also a huge loss of identity. My identity was wrapped up in the sport. I was on the couch for a couple of months, really depressed. Not having a direction or a plan of what I was going to do that day.

While I trained and competed at a high level in competitive sailing it just wasn't possible to have a job and compete at the same time because my world was travel. We were away, for the better part of six months of the year, on and off, back and forth, so to do anything else was tough. I also knew that if I wasn't putting in full time effort, I wasn't going to get the results I wanted. So, I left a fifteen-year career in marketing (I was forty when I competed in Beijing) to pursue my goal.

I was super lucky because my mom bumped into this lady who was a business coach. She told her that if I needed some guidance after the games to give her a call. If I didn't have her, I think I would have been much worse off.

It was months before I was ready to get in touch with her. I had tried to find a job on my own, but the problem was I had spent the last five years training to go to the Olympic Games, and there are very few people who gave a shit. What she did was help me put my sport experience into business terms. It was a challenging process for me. She had to push me really hard to understand the relatable skills. She had me write down everything I did when I was competing and training then she helped me translate that into what employers are looking for.

I was so panicked, and I would argue with her, "No, I'm not that person, I don't want to do this. I don't know who I am." I was so unsure of myself that I had friends who would offer put in a good word for me if their company was hiring. And I remember thinking I don't want to take a job that a friend of mine has recommended me for because I'm going to hurt their reputation by taking this job.

How I describe this time of my life was like being in grade nine on steroids. You're at the top of the school in grade eight and then you're the "minor niner." You push, you achieve, you excel, you're at the top and being celebrated. Then you go into a company who values that person and the personality traits that got you there, but then they put you at the bottom. It was difficult to reconcile emotionally.

When I would start to personalize everything and think, *I'm not worthy*, I would pause and say, *Hold on—wait a minute: I've seen this before. I need to reach out to resources who are going to help me get through this.*

I was lucky because I sort of knew that this was a part of the process. I had a lot of former Olympians around me for support. I grew up around Olympic athletes—my dad's a two time Olympian. Sailing is a very tight knit community, and I could go to the bar at the Royal Canadian Yacht Club and be in a room with five Olympians and nobody would know it. So, I could just go and sit there, and they literally would just sit with me and either have a beer or whatever and they just know. I don't know how many people are as fortunate to have that kind of community.

Lately I keep getting asked what is play for me? What do I do for fun? For me it's not "fun," per se, it's competition. Competition is gratifying and satisfying to me. I don't really know what play is. Just talking about my career right now I can feel the adrenaline starting to go. And you're like, yeah, this is the feeling that I like. It's the God piece for me.

When I stopped competing, I lost how to feed my adrenaline needs. It's almost like an addiction. When you lose your source of where you get that fix, you're lost – where are you going to get it again? Are you going to get it again? Are you going to get it in business? Are you going to get it in some other sports? Where is that going to come from? Recently I decided I want to learn how to play pickleball and, of course, I want to win at pickleball.

I still participate in the sailing community. It's important to me to be part of the community, the culture, just the experience. In sailing, you can get involved in so many different ways that I'm helping to organize the racing. I'm helping to create that at my Sailing Club. Which is actually allowing me the opportunity to be a race official, in places like Bermuda. I want to go it beyond what I'm doing now, which keeps me involved and that's been a good outlet now.

OPPORTUNITY (REMINDER)

Making the change is not an overnight thing but it doesn't have to be a long painful process either. Now that you understand what is going on you can be more conscious about your decisions moving forward to feed yourself in the way that will have you live the post-sports life you want.

The way to trigger your body to make the change is deliberately flooding your body a new emotion (yes—to get addicted to if you want to look at it that way). Spend time everyday focusing on feeling the way you want to primarily feel—love, joy, abundant etc. Focus on feeling it throughout your whole body. If you lose focus gently bring it back but don't move on to anything else in your day until you feel it everywhere even if it's just for a few seconds to start. It's a great practice to start and end your day with.

I know many of you will probably want to choose the same thing that was there: winning and being an awesome warrior (or some flavour of that). The problem is that the level of intensity you are used to feeling it at isn't possible on an everyday basis without being in competitive sport—which you aren't in anymore. To dial it down to a lower level isn't as easy as feeding your cells with something else.

Lastly, if after hearing all of that and making it this far into the book and you still making excuses that you can make it work then YOU ARE STUCK IN YOUR ADDICTION. It is your addiction talking, desiring more and willing to do anything to get it. Now is the time to apply your will and trust that your way forward is through choosing something new.

PART III

SPIRIT

"I just have to feel like there's some element of victory in something that I'm doing."

- Tony Jackson (Professional Basketball Player)

CHAPTER 7

IDENTITY CRISIS: NAVIGATING THE JOURNEY TO SELF-IDENTITY IN RETIREMENT

CHALLENGE

Through all my research this is one that comes up as the biggest challenge that every retired athlete has to face. NFL vice president of player engagement and former Pro Bowl cornerback Troy Vincent has said *"Every athlete has to face the same question when they're done: 'Who am I?'"*

You have spent a lifetime identifying yourself as a hockey player, gymnast, runner, (insert your sport here). And not just as an athlete, but as *an elite* athlete at the head of your field. Now that your career has come to an end, you're left sitting there with that overwhelming question of who you are.

The problem is that you defined yourself as your job—not just in language but as an identity. In other words, you've made it literally mean that YOU are your work. So now that your job is over, you are over. The loss of identity can easily consume someone from the inside. Without a sense of self, it can feel like your life has no purpose and can open the door for mental health problems. Everyone around you has had many years to figure out who they are while you struggle to redefine yourself and catch up to everyone else. It can be very alienating, and many suffer in silence as they search for their way out to a new identity.

OPPORTUNITY

This is an amazing opportunity for self-reflection that not many people get to engage in outside of a mid-life crisis. It is important to remember that YOU were never that thing. YOU were someone who did that thing. Just as I am not a coach, coaching is something that I do. Now you get to purposefully look across your life at the myriad things you've done and pull out all the common threads. Those common threads are the indicators of the true YOU. It's important to look at your individual qualities that got you to the top levels of your sport.

With all the athletes that I have coached, interviewed, or had the privilege of chatting with, the one thing that is the same is that the qualities they each possessed that enabled them to compete at the highest levels was different. Those qualities are a good indicator of who YOU are, more so than the fact that you were a pro athlete or a champion. I remember talking to a former pro football player who had gone through a similar exercise and said that he realized that a key trait was that HE was a winner. He would do whatever was necessary to win. He took that and applied it deliberately in many areas to enrich his life.

CHOOSING A DIFFERENT TUNE:
HOW ROSANNA FOUND SIGNIFICANCE BEYOND WATER POLO

I remember I bought a little guitar—called a guitalele—to take with me to Shanghai. I had just bought it, and the next day at practice my coach says, "Don't bring your guitar—no music while you're traveling. I want you focused." I had other ambitions for my life than just sport, and my concern was that staying in sport for too long would get in the way of me doing other things. Being reprimanded really brought that to the forefront.

I was a water polo player, and we spent several hours per day at the pool, kind of like a full-time job. I began feeling a pull to do something else because I have many passions. Not everyone is that way, but it's always been a part of my personality. I felt like if I was choosing water polo then I wasn't choosing something else. That's really when I said, "Okay, I'm retiring after 2012, no matter what happens." In 2008, I was considering retiring after that Olympic cycle and then we just missed the Olympics, and I still felt the fire. So, I decided to go for another cycle, until I I'd be twentieth. Regardless of what happened, I had set my end date. That was actually really positive for me, psychologically, because even on a really bad day I'd just say to myself, "Honour your word and finish when you said you were going to finish" versus "screw this, I'm mad at everything so I'm going to quit now".

In our qualifying run for 2012, we ended up just missing the Olympics in the twentieth round of sudden death penalty shots at the Pan American Games. We then went to Europe and lost a game that would have qualified us by one goal. And that was it. My coach hardly played me in that final European tournament. I had no idea this was how the end of my career would play out.

Not only did the team not qualify, but as an individual, it was super upsetting for me to end my athletic career hardly playing in the tournament that was our last chance. I was mad, and I didn't go back to practices once we got home. I was like, "I'm done. I guess retirement's coming early." I knew I was retiring regardless, and if they were going to take away my carding money because I didn't go to some stupid practices just to say I went for a few months, then fine. I was bitter. I didn't second guess my decision to retire at all, however. I was angry at having given so much for all of those years and then that was how it ended.

Since I was eight, I was a pretty devout Christian and when I retired, I still was one. I did have a deep faith that helped me get through not achieving a dream I'd worked at for fourteen years. I trusted that it wasn't all for nothing, and that I could leave water polo for the next chapter of my life. I went for something, I gave it my all, and even though I didn't get my goal, I certainly transformed as a person. It's like, go for the stuff that's most important to you, and whether you get it or not, who you become will be the achievement.

Overall, sport made me feel significant. Then I transitioned to music, and it was kind of neat to some people because I was a former athlete doing music. That also made me feel significant. I think I was always chasing significance through my achievements because my parents weren't super present to validate me.

When I was truly loved by my husband, I got a different type of significance, and it took away a lot of the desire to be special in the eyes of the world, whether through sport or music. Today, almost ten years after I've retired, one of my teammates is still playing, and I think it's great because she truly loves the sport. My reason for doing sport wasn't totally pure, and I think there are probably a bunch of athletes like me. What part is pure love of that thing, and what part is just seeking significance? I was able to see it much more clearly as time went on. Sport made me feel significant. That's why I pursued it. It was definitely a healthier option than drugs or a whole bunch of other things, so I'm still super grateful it was my path.

My journey as an athlete really gave me grit, discipline, and a canvas to look at my emotions every day. Dealing with the craziness of being human, feeling all these emotions, and then having to go to practice because I'd made a commitment really developed my character. Some mornings before practice I'd think it was the end of the world, but then three hours later after practice I'd be giggling with my teammates in a completely different state of mind. What a lesson to not mope in my shit and just go do some exercise! I'm eternally grateful for that lesson. I can't thank it enough. Reflecting on this makes me so happy that I get to serve the sport community still today because if I didn't have sport in my life, I don't know who I'd be.

I would tell others to take confidence in all you learned in your athletic career because it's super valuable: working toward a goal and having grit and following through on your word is very valuable in the corporate world.

For work, I've had a positive experience because of what I bring to the table as a person. I went from never having a corporate job into a director position from doing a consulting role. They said whatever characteristics I gained in my life outside of the corporate world, they're very valuable here. It doesn't matter what you did or if you're missing some technical skills, character is still half of the equation. Don't underestimate that and really take pride in all you became in your journey as an athlete.

OPPORTUNITY (REMINDER)

This is an amazing opportunity for self-reflection that not many people get to engage in outside of a mid-life crisis. It is important to remember that YOU were never that thing. YOU were someone who did that thing. Just as I am not a coach, coaching is something that I do. Now you get to purposefully look across your life at the myriad things you've done and pull out all the common threads. Those common threads are the indicators of the true YOU. It's important to look at your individual qualities that got you to the top levels of your sport.

With all the athletes that I have coached, interviewed, or had the privilege of chatting with, the one thing that is the same is that the qualities they each possessed that enabled them to compete at the highest levels was different. Those qualities are a good indicator of who YOU are, more so than the fact that you were a pro athlete or a champion. I remember talking to a former pro football player who had gone through a similar exercise and said that he realized that a key trait was that HE was a winner. He would do whatever was necessary to win. He took that and applied it deliberately in many areas to enrich his life.

CHAPTER 8

SHIFTING THE COMPASS: BUILDING A NEW SENSE OF PURPOSE

CHALLENGE

For most of your life you've had pretty much one goal, one purpose: make it to the big show in your sport. If you made it there, then you likely turned your attention to how to stay on top. This is your purpose and your passion, to be the best athlete you can be. This purpose is all consuming and dictates everything else in your life. That's what it takes to be the best of the best.

When you retire, that purpose is suddenly gone, and you can be left feeling directionless or wondering why you're here. Many believe that they need to figure out a 'new' purpose in order to move forward in their life. Unfortunately, this deep self-analysis work can be a silent killer keeping you in one spot for too long as you can also get wrapped up in the feeling of loss around your identity and purpose (essentially a state of mourning) or consumed by finding what your new purpose is. The question is, how do you find another reason for living as soon as possible to keep you moving?

OPPORTUNITY

People can spend a lifetime searching for their "purpose." The big secret is that you have no divine purpose per se, one defining why what you were put on this earth to do. There are things that you connect with on deep levels that inspire you and drive you – that give you a *sense* of purpose. This can be more than one thing and it can change over time.

Steve Jobs' purpose wasn't to create Apple Computers. He connected to the idea of the personal computer on a very deep way that inspired him and drove him. When you retired, you didn't lose your purpose, you lose your *sense* of purpose The opportunity here is to be grateful—any opportunity you have to be grateful is a good one—that you've been able to experience such a strong sense of purpose, because very few people do. It's important to recognise this because, to be perfectly honest, you may never find something that makes you feel like that again. The best way to look at it is you've been there, done that, bought the t-shirt, and now it's time to move on to new experiences. If you can do this, then you will be freed up to experience new things as they come and see where new opportunities will take you.

Take the heavy expectation of "it has to be as good or better than" off the table and choose to enjoy fully whatever it is you are doing now. Fulfillment does not come from external sources (positions, titles, or awards), it comes from within and your own sense of peace and acceptance with who you are and the life you have chosen for yourself. This is your opportunity to build a new compass and point it in whatever direction you choose with no expectations other than to enjoy the ride.

Give up your expectations that your purpose, or what you do, has to look or be a certain way. Start experiencing life and noticing what you enjoy, what lights you up and what makes you feel good about yourself. These are the breadcrumbs to finding another strong sense of purpose. The key here is to just keep moving. Keep doing something, anything, and don't take heaps of time to figure out what your new *raison d'etre* is. You never got anywhere by just standing still.

KNOWING WHEN TO EXIT:
TONY'S JOURNEY FROM THE HARDWOOD TO PERSONAL TRIUMPHS

I played professional basketball at the time when it was starting to go into a "golden age" type of thing. Michael Jordan was big. The game was going global. I played pretty much everywhere; the only continent I didn't play in was Africa. I played in the inauguration season of the Chinese Basketball Association (CBA). I had kind of a Forrest Gump type career, where I did things that at the time, I never thought were great. But when I look back on it, I think, wow, you know.

Playing overseas, you sign year to year, so you don't know what's happening the next year. I knew at some point that I wanted to have a family [but] I didn't want to have a family and be doing this. I didn't want to be one of these guys that didn't know what to do or who I was after basketball. I didn't have a clue what that was going to be, but it was always on my mind. I was about twenty-six at that time. I said that if I had to have major surgery, or I got too old or [was] not making enough money, then I would call it quits. I knew I didn't want to play into my forties.

After a couple years, I ended up in Australia and my knees were starting to give me some issues and I knew I had injured it, but not enough that I needed surgery. I could still play but I knew I was injured. Surgery would rectify the situation but like I said to myself, if I had to get surgery I was going to call it quits so I just played as long as I could.

I wasn't one hundred percent when I played my last few years, and I told my agent at the time that I wanted to be closer to home. Australia was just too far away to come home regularly (Christmas, off-season etc.). So, I told my agent to look for something in Brazil. And if I couldn't get a certain amount of money then I would call it quits.

He tried. He couldn't get anything for me in Brazil. So, I went back to Australia for a second season. After that season, I said, okay, try Brazil again. He got me somewhere north of Brazil, but I wanted to be in Brazil. I said, okay, well, no, I'm going home. If something comes up within the next year, maybe I'll consider it.

I came home and then had to make that transition, the psychological transition and everything like that. In my mind. I had to face the reality that the call was probably not going to come. I was twenty-nine at that time and decided to stop training. I didn't go to the gym for a year. I knew if I went to the gym, I would probably get that itch. I would start calling around and I didn't want to do that. I stayed away for an entire year, but in the back of my mind I was hoping for that call, but the call never came.

Watching that first NBA pre-season and not playing just brought back so many memories. At that time, I knew pretty much all the guys. I'd either met them, partied with them, played against them, or played with them at Magic's pickup games at UCLA or the NBA summer league. Seeing them play, a part of me was wishing that I was still in the mix. I think the part that I missed was the camaraderie, the talking with them. And the locker room. I missed the competitiveness of setting a goal with a group of guys and banding together to go to war with guys and accomplish something. That's what I missed way more than the game itself.

When I resurfaced after that first year, I started going to the gym. I think one of the first places I went to was the YMCA downtown, where a bunch of locals were playing ball. But my timing was off. Like, it was the first time that I realized how important timing was. And, you know, the tendencies, the instinctual muscle memory, and things like it. That is when I realized how important it was because I didn't have it anymore. And watching guys that just weren't even close to the level that I had played at and them feeling that they were relevant, and me getting frustrated, because I knew that in my mind, they're not relevant as far as the competitive level, but I couldn't back what my mind was telling me. So, there was that aspect of the physical change. The mental aspect, I 'now that

I'm just a competitive person by nature. I had to find other releases and started putting that competitive element into things at work and coaching the next generation. I just have to feel like there's some element of victory in something that I'm doing.

So, am I happier now, or when I played ball? I definitely say happier now. I have a lot to live for. I feel more accomplished. When I played ball, I was thinking, there's no way I'm gonna beat this, like money's coming in fast and I'm going wherever I want to go. I'm hanging out with celebrities and people are treating me like a celebrity. I had those perks in the countries that I played in. When the lights are on and you're on the stage, I could see how some people can lose themselves in that and at some points of my playing career I did. You become entitled because you have a status; you have expectations about how you want to be treated.

But the uncertainty of what comes after, I was thinking, wow, okay. The first couple of years, it was kind of like, okay, I don't know how this is going to go. But then I established my own family network, I got married and divorced. I had my son and my daughter. I also raised two other boys as my own. So, to me, just watching how you helped shape another human being from birth till whatever—I don't know what beats that. That's what I found where my passion is, you know, and that's why I go back to that thing. We all have our goals and things in life that we want. But if I were asked, what would I trade? I would trade more for this, but I wouldn't trade this for anything.

OPPORTUNITY (REMINDER)

People can spend a lifetime searching for their "purpose." The big secret is that you have no divine purpose per se, one defining why what you were put on this earth to do. There are things that you connect with on deep levels that inspire you and drive you – that give you a *sense* of purpose. This can be more than one thing and it can change over time.

Steve Jobs' purpose wasn't to create Apple Computers. He connected to the idea of the personal computer on a very deep way that inspired him and drove him. When you retired, you didn't lose your purpose, you lose your *sense* of purpose The opportunity here is to be grateful—any opportunity you have to be grateful is a good one—that you've been able to experience such a strong sense of purpose, because very few people do. It's important to recognise this because, to be perfectly honest, you may never find something that makes you feel like that again. The best way to look at it is you've been there, done that, bought the t-shirt, and now it's time to move on to new experiences. If you can do this, then you will be freed up to experience new things as they come and see where new opportunities will take you.

Take the heavy expectation of "it has to be as good or better than" off the table and choose to enjoy fully whatever it is you are doing now. Fulfillment does not come from external sources (positions, titles, or awards), it comes from within and your own sense of peace and acceptance with who you are and the life you have chosen for yourself. This is your opportunity to build a new compass and point it in whatever direction you choose with no expectations other than to enjoy the ride.

Give up your expectations that your purpose, or what you do, has to look or be a certain way. Start experiencing life and noticing what you enjoy, what lights you up and what makes you feel good about yourself. These are the breadcrumbs to finding another strong sense of purpose. The key here is to just keep moving. Keep doing something, anything, and don't take heaps of time to figure out what your new *raison d'etre* is. You never got anywhere by just standing still.

CHAPTER 9

EMBRACING THE VOID:
TRANSFORMING LOSS INTO OPPORTUNITY

CHALLENGE

One day you're an elite athlete the next day you're not. The training regimen has stopped, there's no one telling you what to do anymore, there's no more team, no more coach, no more sponsors, no more celebrity status. You're left with the distinct feeling of a void in your life – clearly something that was a part of you is now missing.

Everything that you dedicated your life to, believed yourself to be, and lived and breathed for most of your life is gone. The YOU that you knew yourself to be has essentially died and what's left in its place is a massive void. The challenge is to manage this feeling of emptiness that you've been left with, and how to fill it in a way that pulls your life forward in the direction you want it to go.

OPPORTUNITY

The opportunity is that you get to fill that void with whatever you desire. Many people must work hard to carve out even a little space mentally, physically, and emotionally to make room for new things or directions in their life. Most won't even try because unconsciously they are too scared to let go of parts of their old self that have become so ingrained in their identity. You get to start fresh, recreating who you want to be.

Recognise your retirement as a time of death and rebirth like a phoenix rising from the ashes. Give yourself a short time to mourn, then celebrate who you were and get excited about who you are becoming. Be deliberate in your choices on what direction you want your life to take. Utilize all the talents and mental strength you gained as an athlete (your transferrable skills) to make it all happen.

THE FIGHT BEYOND THE RING: IBRAHIM'S FIGHT TO FIND PURPOSE

In boxing we have a saying, "it's the punch that you don't see."

I have never been hurt in a fight, except my last. But I've never been stunned in a fight. I felt the punches to the body where I'm like, *Oh no, asshole, that hurt!* But never dazed or anything like that. So, nothing really clicked into my mind until my doctor said that I've actually had thousands of mini concussions over my career. Anytime that I'd seen "stars" or lost feelings in my legs, that was a mini one. For me, that was normal. That happened almost every sparring session. Concussions happen when you're moving one way and then the punch comes when you don't expect it and your brain is still traveling in that other direction. It hits against your skull and gets bruised essentially.

In sparring that was a norm. When I was competing, it was against somebody my weight whereas sparring I'm sparring with a lot of heavier guys, pros, amateurs, high level guys. From eleven years old I was always sparring with older, heavier kids, and as I got older and obviously got stronger and better, I started sparring with heavier guys who were on the national teams or pros. They'd try to hold back but sparring sessions can get heated, I'd hit them, they want to hit me back to keep me off of them.

I got lucky that I was offered an opportunity to take part in a concussion study and went in for a research MRI (a much more rigorous scan). Going into the doctor's office, I figured I just needed to take a couple months off then get back at it. But man, when the doctor showed me the scans of what a normal brain looks like, and what mine looked like I couldn't believe it. All those little things from all of those fights and sparring sessions never went away. They just kept adding up.

I can be stubborn at times and not level-headed, but something made sense. Even as much as I wanted to fight it, I thought, *I should just go with it – right?* The one thing that's very sad to see in boxing is you see a lot of guys as they get older dementia or punch-drunk syndrome starts kicking in. This wasn't about taking some time off this was time to look into something else.

I was a carded athlete here in Canada. What that means is I would get a stipend from Government of Canada. The way it worked was for me to keep my card I'd have to go to the Canadian championships. If I didn't win it, there goes my carding. That's $2000 a month, plus school tuition, plus all the physio, plus my international trips for competitions, that's almost $150,000. So, the first thing I thought when I retired was, *shit, where am I gonna get cash now?*

I didn't really go to school to get anything, so I don't have a degree or a trade or anything like that. So, whatever I could find, I would do. I literally worked every kind of job you can even think of. I was working at a warehouse; I was doing some boxing classes at a local gym and some personal training; I was literally on Craigslist looking for anything to do.

Luckily, I ended up getting into Canada Post so that helped alleviate a very big stressor.

But I still have that competitive drive. Every day at work (my job is piece-work—so I am not there for a set amount of time) if I finish my route that is supposed to take eight in five hours, I get paid for the eight. Then I would do overtime. Within my eight hours, I'd finish my route and take out another route. That's how I would challenge myself. Many times, I would even overbook myself, I'd have the commitment to be at the gym and I'll take some overtime and then I'll sprint down to gym. My wife hates it, but I make it on time to the gym literally walking in with about two minutes before my class starts.

My biggest challenge is mental stimulation. That's still a missing in some ways though I've gotten better at handling it. It led to me drinking a bit more and smoking though I've quit smoking now. But it caused a big strain on my relationship. Literally, it was just out of sheer boredom. My wife thought I was an alcoholic for a bit because I'd come home at one o'clock if overtime was dry at work and there was nothing to do. I would sit at home until she came home and finish a six pack of beer—and still want to drink more. Looking back, I think maybe I should have joined a sport of some sort, or maybe even a gym membership. At the time I couldn't see it. It's important to find a way to channel all of this mental energy. It's something I'm still going through and dealing with but making progress every day for me is the key.

OPPORTUNITY (REMINDER)

The opportunity is that you get to fill that void with whatever you desire. Many people must work hard to carve out even a little space mentally, physically, and emotionally to make room for new things or directions in their life. Most won't even try because unconsciously they are too scared to let go of parts of their old self that have become so ingrained in their identity. You get to start fresh, recreating who you want to be.

Recognise your retirement as a time of death and rebirth like a phoenix rising from the ashes. Give yourself a short time to mourn, then celebrate who you were and get excited about who you are becoming. Be deliberate in your choices on what direction you want your life to take. Utilize all the talents and mental strength you gained as an athlete (your transferrable skills) to make it all happen.

CHAPTER 10

BEING OK WITH THE UNFINISHED: FINDING CLOSURE AND WHOLENESS SO YOU CAN MOVE ON POWERFULLY

CHALLENGE

You may have chosen to leave your sport, or you may have injured out. Either way, many people feel their career was incomplete. There are often regrets that you didn't accomplish more. Even if you feel like it was time for you to retire, I challenge you to look deeper and see if you really are complete with, or at peace with, everything that was and wasn't in your career.

This incompleteness, which often shows up as a longing for more time or one more chance, can simmer for years, diminishing the vitality of the new life you're creating. It's like you have one foot in your old life and one foot in the new.

OPPORTUNITY

This is an opportunity to start fresh by completing your career. Completing is when you spend some time looking back at all your experiences and letting go of any could haves, should haves, and wishes, with gratitude for what you did accomplish. That's not to say that the old you is no longer part of your life and to never think about it again. It's just that it will no longer have a say in what you are doing now or in the future. So many of us move from one job, career, or relationship to another without spending a moment deliberately completing our experience.

THE PURSUIT OF PASSION: MARK'S JOURNEY TO BUILDING A LEGACY AFTER TRACK AND FIELD

After the Seoul Olympics I was done. Retired, never wanted to see track again. Never wanted to do it, I was fed up with the system, I was fed up with everything. I wanted nothing more to do with it. I was suspended for two years, I was injured and had an Achilles operation, which for athletes, is the worst operation you can have, especially for hurdlers and sprinters. I couldn't walk. I had just bought a whole bunch of real estate because "I was gonna win Seoul" of course, and was now in debt up to my eyeballs.

It was just by chance—it was actually a track friend's sister—that changed my mind. She was here in Toronto and my buddy called me up and said, "You know, my sister is going to be there. She's doing some work for a month why don't you hang out with her, show her Toronto a little bit?" We hung out and at the end of it, she said, "why don't you come over to Britain and train with my brother?"

Like I said, at that point, I had zero interest. I was done and done. But I eventually went to Britain, started training, and thought, *maybe I can go for one more.* It was out of my experience of coming back to compete in one more Olympic Games (Atlanta) where I really learned the most about myself, about digging deep. I really had to dig deep to make it happen and find out who I am. You don't come back from something like Seoul unless you really know yourself and know what you want.

After the Atlanta Olympics, it was funny, I was at a wedding. I was sitting at a table with some people, and they're like, "Mark, what are you going to do now that you're retired?" I didn't know I was retired.

I competed so pathetically in Atlanta that I guess they figured my career was over, and it didn't even occur to me. It was like, *Ouch! Thanks, a lot people. I guess I'm gonna have to find something else to do.* It wasn't really a hard-stop retirement, it was more of a transition into thinking, okay, what do I do now, because all I've done my whole life, even when I went to university for seven years. I really wasn't there for school. I was there because that was the best place to train. So, I really hadn't thought about doing anything else.

Even when I did eventually retire, I continued to go back over to Britain to help coach and train with my buddy, Colin. Funny enough, the first thing I told him later on is "Colin, wanna know the best thing you can do as an athlete? Don't retire." Because as an athlete you pour your heart and soul for years and years and years, and the more successful you get, the more work you have to do to get there. It's like, there's nothing else you can do – there's nothing else you want to do. There was no career waiting for me, I wasn't going to be a doctor or whatever. There was nothing else. Track and field were all I knew. I was just really, really lucky that I was successful, because you can parlay a gold medal into a lot of things.

Unfortunately, even winning the gold medal, especially in this country, doesn't translate to being set for life. If you're in any other country, you could really retire. But here, I never made any money when I was running. And I never made money off the gold medal, there were no sponsorships or anything. I was at the top of my game, best in the world and it meant nothing to anybody except myself and my family.

The first thing I thought was, *okay, I'm done. So, what do I like to do?* I don't know why but I've had this fascination with the martial arts. I even love to watch Bruce Lee and I always wanted to learn the martial arts. I remember watching for hours with a friend. We would sit down and watch the old Bruce Lee movies and we loved that; I don't know why. So, I thought I'm going to do martial arts. I wanted to stay fit and didn't want to do track, I didn't want to run, I didn't want to train I just wanted to do martial arts.

I used to drive from Toronto to Hamilton every day because I found the school that I really liked. One day the instructor says "Mark you're driving forty-five minutes a day to come out here. Why don't you just open your own school?" I said all right, cool. So, I just opened my own school (two schools actually), and I did that for five years.

They were really successful actually. I think the thing that you find with a lot of corporations who hire athletes is because they have the drive. It doesn't matter if you have the talents or skills in that business, they know they can give you that, but they can't give you is that drive it takes to be a high-level athlete. For me I have this drive no matter what it's going to be, no matter what I decide I'm going to do. I'm going to do my best.

The important thing is to know what you want then to put everything into it. I didn't think of myself as being a great athlete or driven or whatever it was, because it's not what I did, it's who I was and who I am now. I still love training. I know it's sort of sort of sick, but I love the pain of training. I still train today and I am sixty years old. I think that's why I have been successful because it's not what I did. This is what I do, this is who I am. I was born to do this. The unfortunate thing is most people don't know what they want.

I'm working with a very successful person in finance. They hate it but they do really well. They make a lot of money but don't enjoy it. They actually hate it, hate the stress etc. The questions I ask them are: What do you want? What do you like? What do you love? They have no idea. Most people don't know, once you find what you love. It's easy. You just do it.

OPPORTUNITY (REMINDER)

This is an opportunity to start fresh by completing your career. Completing is when you spend some time looking back at all your experiences and letting go of any could haves, should haves, and wishes, with gratitude for what you did accomplish. That's not to say that the old you is no longer part of your life and to never think about it again. It's just that it will no longer have a say in what you are doing now or in the future. So many of us move from one job, career, or relationship to another without spending a moment deliberately completing our experience.

CHAPTER 11

A FIGHTER'S JOURNEY: HOW MIRANDA AND IBRAHIM WORKED THROUGH THE STRESSES RETIREMENT CREATED IN THEIR RELATIONSHIP

A few things happened that led to Ibrahim's retirement. His last three fights as a professional were rocky. In his third last fight, it was the first time in his career he ever went down. I never in my life thought he would go down. I guess I saw him as a superhero. When he went down and was unconscious, I'll tell you, that was the most traumatic experience. When he got hurt, I thought, *how could I be at war with this sport that helped me so much?*

I was so angry that he got hurt, and the worst part of boxing and concussions is that he had no memory of going down. He used to watch the replay where he went down, like one hundred times. I would come home, and he'd be replaying it. For me, to this day, I can't watch it. It's too traumatic.

He was starting to see the signs of eighteen years of training, but he didn't want to admit it to himself. Strangely enough, before that fight was the first time he'd ever complained of having a headache and we didn't even think of it at the time. He had told me much later on that at that time he started feeling hits harder from guys that weren't that good.

We all thought that it was a "one off" but then he fought again, and to be honest, it was way too soon. But he won that next fight easily. Then he fought this guy that wasn't nearly as good as he was. During the fight, before Ibrahim was in the fourth round, before he got hurt, his coach said to me, "Miranda, this is it for Ibrahim." He hadn't even lost the fight yet. He ended up losing. It was very stressful in that he went down again from a very easy blow.

Psychologically he knew something's wrong. He'd taken punches from the best in the world and *this* guy put him down. I think the reasoning side kicked in, and he realized it didn't matter what he thought. His athletic ability was slipping. The next day his coach came over and was on the borderline of crying. He told Ibrahim to think about his wife and the life we were building. This is the saddest story. He said, "I believe in you, and you have the potential, but it's time, you have to walk away." To be honest, even then, we both thought no, the fight just happened, let's give it some time.

The deciding factor was the scientific evidence. We got involved in a concussion project, with the leading doctor on concussions in Canada who works with all of the top-level athletes. Ibrahim went in for a research MRI. These are a lot more in depth than a regular MRI. They take about one and a half hours. When the doctor showed us Ibrahim's MRI, it showed spinal cord fluid leaking in his brain. The doctor explained to us that it's basically like an egg and in Ibrahim's case, the egg got cracked. And now no matter what happens, whether it's a slip and fall, whether it's a street fight, anything, his brain is now cracked, and it will never heal.

So now every time moving forward that Ibrahim takes a hit it could be dangerous. Muhammad Ali had it, Sugar Ray Leonard had it, these are things that are Parkinson indicators. They'd never seen it in an athlete so young, because most boxers don't have access to research MRIs. When we saw what a normal brain looks like, and this is what his brain looks like. He said, "That's it."

The most concerning thing is that he would've passed a regular MRI and been able to get his pro boxing license. Most commissions worldwide require an annual CT scan or an MRI for your pro boxing license. That's why you see some boxers really getting hurt, taken out by stretcher, sometimes not waking up. They passed all the necessary tests, including the standard MRI and were deemed fit enough for competition. It's one of those things that yes, they are okay, but at the same time they may not be okay.

He'd beaten some of the best fighters in the world, but there was no way he could beat this. His time was up. I thank God Ibrahim was married because I think if he wasn't, he would have been like so many other boxers that continue until they can't talk, or they have other long-term problems, because your brain can only take so much. It also helped that around the same time he had started to talk about how he was tired and just wanted a regular life. He was just tired, tired of training two times a day, his contract was in Montreal, I was in Toronto, tired of not eating at barbecues, tired of constantly being away from his family, constantly just having to sacrifice so much.

But I'll be honest: when he first retired it was a gong show; he couldn't sit still. There's no way he could have any type of office job. I pushed him to get out of the house and do something, anything. The concern was that he went from training twice a day to not wanting to do anything. No running, no walking, no weights, nothing. He wasn't interested in eating healthy either. He just went totally off the rails. I found it extremely difficult because in general I'm a healthy person. I eat healthy, I get good sleep,

I don't drink too much, I don't smoke. But he went off the train, so he was drinking and smoking and whatever else, like a kid in a candy store. He had never had this amount of freedom. He grew up with a strict Muslim upbringing where you're not supposed to drink, you're not supposed to do all these things.

It's like I married an athlete and then I got a rock star or something. And it got progressively worse. In the beginning I made excuses like, *okay, he's going through a transition.* We were very compatible but then all of a sudden, I was married to someone I didn't know because everything that linked us didn't exist. I didn't understand who this person was. Thank God for Canada Post because he got on as a mailman. The blessing of that is that it was manual labour. He's carrying heavy bags, walking twenty kilometers a day in the cold and heat and he has a very good work ethic. So that helped start to drain the energy because he was really struggling with just the amount of excess energy he had.

The thing is when Ibrahim retired in terms of athletic ability, he was at his prime, but his brain had eighteen years of impact. I tried to get him involved in crossover sports like elite level rowing. But he just was uninterested in any type of training. Four years later he started drinking and smoking a lot more. He used to say, "I'm drinking because I'm bored." I think that's when we started to struggle even more. I realized that things were going downhill, but I didn't really see it. At work he was getting less over time, so he was coming home with more free time.

We moved our business from downtown to north of the city, so he could no longer just come to the gym after his shift, so he was working less with the kids and the athletes. He was always a goal setter and set goals every year, then he decided he was no longer interested. He thought that every goal he set never came true. So, he stopped setting any goals. I couldn't handle it and had no idea what to do so I went to therapy. Because I didn't understand, I didn't know how to be in this relationship because I married an apple, and I got an orange. And the orange wouldn't go to therapy. He wouldn't accept it. He refused to change. He just kept on this complete rampage and then in all honesty, we separated earlier this year. I told him he had to decide to either stop drinking, or move out, those are the only two options. I couldn't deal with it anymore. So, he moved out. I was not expecting that.

But then one of our dogs died. The weirdest thing about this is for Ibrahim it was the best thing that could have happened because for the first time in his thirty-five years, he cried, and he cried a lot. It was two days of complete crying. He used to think something was wrong with him because he thought he couldn't cry. He was kind of brought up in a traumatic environment and boxing was like his safe space. When he was in the ring, he felt safe, he felt like that's his destiny and he's in control of it. But for some reason, when our dog died, it's like all of this deep emotional stuff that he'd been holding on to, like us not being able to have kids, not going to the Olympics, all that started to wash away.

Later that year I told him he could move home but he'd have to give up drinking. To be honest, the hardest part for me is even now I don't understand because with Ibrahim when he was an athlete, during Ramadan or before fights he never drank. But as soon as he lost that commitment to his sport, the drinking just got out of control. It's like he had no reason to stop.

But the weird thing is, this is the part I still don't understand is all the time that we were separated, he drank almost every day, smoked every day. Then all of a sudden, he's home now and he doesn't drink at all. And I'm like, do you have, like, withdrawal symptoms? Are you okay? He says he's totally fine. I talked to my athletic therapist about it, he said to be honest, I think Ibrahim's drinking has more to do with his concussions, and the process of what boxing has done to him than him just being like an asshole.

I don't know if that's the case, but you have to keep in mind that he's had a lot of hits to the head. The other thing that sucks about boxing is that

Ibrahim had one hundred twenty-three amateur fights, one hundred nine wins, twelve professional fights, two losses, but the whole world only cares that he got knocked out. In that fight he even knocked the guy down twice, but his whole career is now not important. It was like his eighteen-year career got defined in ten seconds. Then there was the relationship stuff in terms of us not being able to have kids and the life that we kind of thought we were going to have is not the life that we had, I think all of those things played into it.

But when the dog died, he was able to rid himself of all that hurt and now we're in a really good place. He's in a really good place. He's back to himself, working out, started eating healthy again. It's like to orange is turning back into the apple I married. When he moved out, he started journaling and he started to get all of these memories of his childhood, and certain boxing matches, and I think he started to work through the fact that he had a great athletic career.

He gave it his best, and the cards fell where they did, but he still has a good life, we have a good life. We don't have any illnesses, we're healthy, we don't have our own kids, but we have a charity, we see hundreds of kids a year. We have a little guy that lives with us part time. I think he's better able to now just understand that if I live in that world of the past, I'll just stop moving forward. And now to be honest, Canada Post had its time, but it's like that time ran out.

And even as a part of the concussion project, the doctors were saying, that because he was in a fight or flight mode for eighteen years, his brain feels stagnant now. So, they told him to pick up a language, or go back to university. He needs to get the brain pumping, because he's been in essentially overdrive for his whole life and now his brain is going dormant. Canada Post is labour, it's not challenging him, he's a very smart guy. Now he's going through the process to be a Border Services Agent. I just think that the task of having to pass tests and going to get certifications, has helped him mentally and emotionally. I feel it's almost like he wanted all or nothing and now he's starting to realize that you can have the good and you can do the training and you can be a little bit in it without feeling like you have to be the Michael Jordan or Magic Johnson.

When I look back over the years that he has been retired I think it really all comes down to kindness for both for each other and understanding the world that Ibrahim had been in for eighteen years. That doesn't change just because the doctor says there's a little break in your brain.

Now, we both have a goal of going to the Olympics with an athlete that we created from our club. Ibrahim truly enjoys refereeing so he does a lot of refereeing and judging. But I will say definitely he didn't really deal with retirement until now. It was like he put it in a bag, and he just never opened the bag.

PART IV
PUTTING IT INTO ACTION

CHAPTER 12

SHAPING YOUR NEW WORLD: CRAFTING YOUR ENVIRONMENTS TO ELEVATE YOUR LIFE

"Where the sports system fails athletes is in understanding what they're creating, besides somebody that can jump really high or run really fast or sail a boat. At the end of the day, who cares? I never go sailing anymore, it's just totally unimportant to me. But all of the other experiences that I got are massively important."

– Chris Cook

One aspect that I haven't spoken about yet is your environment—the people, places, and things that you surround yourself with. For most of your life you have worked to create an environment around you that supported you as a top-level athlete. What that means is that everything and everyone around you has been chosen by you to remind you of the attributes that you believed you had to embody to be at the top of your sport. If you had a strong belief that you must sacrifice a lot to be the best, the people around you expect you to miss events in order to train.

This environment was a great thing right up until you retired. Your environment is still working to remind you – push you – to embody those attributes of who you were. Changes need to be made to support who you are now and your new goals in life. If your environment isn't changed to reflect your new goals, then it's going to make it hard to make changes stick. It may be an extreme example but it's on point. This is the same thing that happens to people who go into rehab facilities for substance addiction they do really well at the facility but if they don't change aspects of their home environment, they are more likely to relapse (Research shows there is a direct correlation between your environment and likelihood of relapse).

Though some or many of your old attributes or beliefs may be great for your life moving forward they all should be re-examined and the ones that no longer serve you should be removed, and your new ones added. This means having conversations with family and friends about how they can support you best moving forward and what attributes you no longer wish to keep. It may also require removing things from your physical environment that are a reminder of embodying those old attributes. Your new environment should be one that supports and pulls for you to be you just as your old one did. Your new environments should focus on you not as an athlete or anything else but the beautiful, awesome, whole and complete person that you are.

RENOVATE YOUR ENVIRONMENTS

This section will guide you through a step-by-step process I created that will have you look at all aspects of your life in a clear and organized way to help you draw your own conclusions on what works and doesn't work in your life anymore. Then once you are aware of what works and doesn't work you can choose what to keep and what to let go of (Hint: let go of the things that aren't pulling you forward in the new direction of your life). Not just the big stuff like your home or your job or your friends but what you watch, listen to, follow, eat and put on your body (including your underwear) are all included. All these areas (and many more) make up the multiple layers of your overall environment and experience of the world.

There is your outermost environment where the people and things that you have little regular interaction with reside, your intermediate environment which are people and things that you aren't as close to but they are around you none the less on a weekly basis, and lastly your immediate environment where all the people and things closest to you usually on an almost daily basis are. All these have a significant impact on your experience of life at any given moment and therefore none should be weighed less than another. The main difference between them is the amount of time it takes to negatively affect you.

JOY AND HAPPINESS ARE NOT THE SAME THING

There is actually a distinct difference between Happiness and Joy. Simply put, Joy is a state greater than Happiness. It's like happiness squared or cubed. It's an all-encompassing deep feeling that just resonates through your whole body and is therefore used sparingly by people because many, in fact, are unsure they have had such an experience. Let me tell you when you've had a joyous moment you know it! The trick is to hang on to the things that empower you to move forward and lose the things that get you stuck in the past.

From here on in our focus is on the big prize – Joy

PART IV
WORKSHEETS

CHAMPION'S BLUEPRINT: CURATING WINNING ENVIRONMENTS FOR HAPPINESS AND FULFILLMENT

On a theoretical level it's obvious that you shouldn't keep things around you that are going to hold you back from achieving what you want to achieve – kind of a no brainer right? I'll never forget when I first got this concept. I was watching a Jack Canfield seminar which brought up the concept you are a median of your 5 closest friends. Something I pride myself on is my openness to trying out new concepts to see how or if they fit in my life before passing judgement on them. This was not one of those cases. It's one of the few things that I called bullshit on immediately. I refused to look deeper because I knew I was 'achieving' (meaning a fuller, richer life – and of course all B.S.) more than my friends. I had done all of this work on myself and went to great depths to clear out my crap so that I could live my life on my terms.

Then it hit me like a punch in the nose. What if I actually spent my time with people who were 'achieving' at a higher level than I was? What would my life be like? Where would I be able to go? What could I do? The people that I was spending the majority of my time with were wonderful beautiful people whom I'd known almost my whole life and there is absolutely nothing wrong with them. But what happened was I had changed. I loved the changes and the direction I was going. If I wanted to keep changing and growing the way I was, then I would need to be around others who were way I was, then I would need to be around others who were also moving in the same direction that I was. So I did – and even took it a step further.

I expanded to concept to include all aspects of life and if something, anything, any person, place or thing didn't bring me joy then it was taking away from the maximum joy I could experience and it had to go. What happened

I created this chapter to guide you through the process that I went through in clear, simple steps. It is to help you see not only what is holding you back but what is possible for yourself when you take the time out to examine what is around you in the various environments that you have created for yourself.

THE SILENT SHAPERS: UNCOVERING THE INFLUENCE OF YOUR OUTERMOST ENVIRONMENT

Personally, I find this environment really fascinating because of how subtle it can be. These are things that largely go unnoticed. You wouldn't even think that they could have any influence on you at all. But they do! At this level it is all about the consistent exposure and its effects on your subconscious.

Your outermost environment consists of:

1. What you see and experience on your way to work.
2. The environment that you have to travel through to get to work.
3. The building/area in which your job is located.
4. The emotional environment of your company.
5. Events that you attend – sporting or concerts (where are you sitting? With the rowdy people or the rich people?)
6. Vacation spots.
7. The city you live in.

Use the chart below to make a list of all of the things in your outermost environment that you are aware of.

MY OUTERMOST ENVIRONMENT

Person, Place, Thing, Event	What way of thinking or being is this <u>environment</u> supporting	Is there a particular phrase that comes to mind when you look at this list as a whole?

BEYOND THE COMFORT ZONE: UNRAVELING THE IMPACT OF YOUR INTERMEDIATE ENVIRONMENT

These are things you are choosing to bring into your life. They tend to be things that you spend a moderate amount of time engaged with on a regular basis (at least weekly). Technically you spend a considerable amount of time in your neighbourhood because your home is in your neighbourhood.

However, your neighbourhood is considered intermediate because it is a place where you spend a moderate amount of time walking around and going to restaurants etc. as opposed to a considerable amount of time in your home – your immediate environment.

Note: It could be argued that your neighbourhood has a great influence on you while in your home. If you feel strongly about that then move it – whatever brings you Joy!

Your intermediate environment consists of:

1. Community/ neighbourhood
2. Social media

3. Hobbies/pastimes

4. Sports

5. Commute by car, transit, cab, carpool

6. Music*

7. Movies*

8. Television*

9. News*

10. Video games

11. Acquaintances

* Depending on frequency of consumption

Use the chart below to make a list of all of the things in your outermost environment that you are aware of.

MY INTERMEDIATE ENVIRONMENT

Person, Place, Thing, Event	What way of thinking or being is this <u>environment</u> supporting	Is there a particular phrase that comes to mind when you look at this list as a whole?

CHAMPION'S SANCTUARY: CULTIVATING BLISS IN YOUR DAILY SPACE

Your immediate environment has one of the greatest impacts on you in the shortest amount of time as it is around you for considerable amounts of time (pretty much daily) and/or you have an emotional attachment to it, i.e., you may not see your best friend every day but your deep connection with them has a large impact on you.

Clothes fall into this category. Even though you don't wear the same thing every day, you have a connection to your clothes, and you make a conscious choice to put a particular thing on your body. Whatever emotion you have connected to that item (even if it is indifference) you are wearing that emotion against your body all day long.

Your immediate environment consists of:

1. Friends, family, significant other
2. Your home
3. Your car
4. Clothes (including socks and underwear)
5. Furniture

6. Jewelry
7. House plants
8. Music (Depending frequency of consumption)
9. Finances
10. Your job and office
11. Your pets
12. Literature

Use the chart below to make a list of all of the things in your outermost environment that you are aware of.

MY IMMEDIATE ENVIRONMENT

Person, Place, Thing, Event	What way of thinking or being is this environment supporting	Is there a particular phrase that comes to mind when you look at this list as a whole?

YOUR INNER ARENA:
WHAT ARE YOU LETTING PAST THE GOALIE?

This is probably the most challenging one to deal with and will be a lifelong pursuit but this one has the biggest and fastest impact on you. Your internal environment is what dictates the state of all of the other environments as it is what causes you to make the choices you make.

The most efficient way to work on this environment is to do personal development courses or one-on-one coaching. It is one of the most powerful things you can do to propel your life forward. I'm not promoting becoming a seminar junkie in any way, shape or form. Listen to your heart when making choices on what work is next for you to do and when it may be time to move on. Seminars and workshops or a great way to learn new tools to help you discover why you do what you do and what you are actually capable of achieving. Take these tools and apply them on your own after the seminar is over on a continual basis so that it becomes a part of your life and not forgotten about after a week or two.

Your Internal environment consists of:

1. **Emotional**
   A. Self-esteem
   B. Emotional balance
   C. Connection to emotions
   D. Creativity
   E. Sexuality (views on sex)

2. **Physical**
   A. Energy level
   B. Strength
   C. Cardiovascular
   D. Endurance
   E. Flexibility
   F. Five senses

3. **Spiritual**
   A. % of time in Ego vs % of time in True Self*
   B. Sense of greater purpose and awareness
   C. Relationship/connection with the Divine (God, Universe etc.)
   D. Understanding and openness to things outside the physical realm
   E. Sense of inner essence or soul
   F. Sense of oneness

4. **Mental**
   A. Thoughts
   B. Attitudes
   C. Beliefs
   D. Values

    E. Concentration

    F. Problem solving

    * See back pages for a chart of differences.

Use the chart below to make a list of all of the things in your internal environment that you are aware of.

Use the chart below to make a list of all of the things in your outermost environment that you are aware of.

MY INTERNAL ENVIRONMENT

Person, Place, Thing, Event	What way of thinking or being is this <u>environment</u> supporting	Is there a particular phrase that comes to mind when you look at this list as a whole?

SO NOW WHAT?

Now that we have established a good working knowledge of these environments it is easy to see how each one in its own way can have a very large impact on you over time. You have subconsciously created each of these environments to reinforce a particular line of thinking about yourself and the world or a way of being.

The big question is when you look at each of the four areas individually are you 100% happy with what you have created and what they support? Chances are no and you're going to lie and say yes because 'it's pretty close'. In this case being close is like being 'kind of pregnant'. Either you are, or you aren't. You are either 100% happy or you aren't. The lying about it is an avoidance mechanism that kicks in when we don't want to deal with our crap in order to get what we've said we wanted for our lives. I call it 'rationalizing happiness'.

So that said, it's damn near impossible to be 100% happy in something as large as an environment that you are in. The best way to look at it is like a game of Jenga. You continually have to remove and replace blocks in order to get you closer to your desired outcome. As you remove blocks, you'll feel unstable because you've been standing on them for so long but unlike Jenga your tower will get more and more stable as you go along. As you progress through life, stop rationalizing happiness and grow who you are, the things that once served you and made you happy may now be the anchors holding you back.

This cycle is an important part of your development and clearing out things that no longer serve you or are pulling you forward is a great habit to get into. The faster you can remove those things the faster you can develop and the more you can exist in Joy.

PUTTING IT INTO PRACTICE

Here's an easy process to follow to you to help you start your detox.

Step 1
Take all of your four lists that you made earlier in the book and organize them this way:

Person, Place, Thing, Event	Does NOT Bring Me Joy	Definitely Brings Me Joy	Could Bring Me Joy

*There is a matching chart for each environment at the end of the book

Step 2
If whatever it is doesn't bring you Joy, then put an 'X' in the 'Does NOT Bring Me Joy' box. If it brings you Joy, then put a check mark in the 'Definitely Brings Me Joy' box. If it could bring you Joy, then put a date for by when you will have recreated it to bring you Joy.

Step 3
I think you know what to do next – let go of the things that do not bring you Joy.

People – In terms of people, look at minimizing the time that you spend with the ones that aren't bringing you Joy and more time with the ones who do.

Commute – If it's your commute to work then change how you get to work (a different route, different transportation etc.).

Job – If it's your job then I think you know what you have to do. There are many different areas that I could go into deeper explanation about what to do to let it go or how to change it but that could be a whole other book.

Home – When it comes to items in your home including your clothes obviously writing down every pair of socks you own would be silly. In your home your task is to go through and give away (either to others or in the case of some items giving it to the garbage) anything and everything that doesn't bring you Joy. This task is HUGE and is the most important as it is a key player in your immediate environment. Set aside an entire weekend to get this done and don't stop until you've finished. You want to rip the band aid off quickly not a little bit every day. That is then torture and doesn't bring anyone Joy (well most of us anyway).

It is easiest to start with all of the random stuff you've accumulated over the years and other less personal items then move to most personal items last when you have some momentum behind you. Be ruthless with yourself there is no item that is exempt from this. That includes socks and underwear. Yes, socks and underwear. The two most over-looked items of clothing that we all wear (well most of us). In the case of your socks, they are mostly seen as utilitarian and therefore don't put any stock into how they look other than the colour and if they have holes (sometimes).

But I guarantee that if you bought yourself some socks that actually brought you Joy – you like the pattern, the material, how they fit, whatever it is for you, it will make a difference in how you feel every day. Underwear could be considered the most intimate piece of clothing that we all put on (well most of us) yet we don't give much thought when purchasing it. For men the big question is "how many are in the package?" for women there tends to be more criteria but do they bring you Joy doesn't tend to be one of them. Sexy and Joy aren't the same thing.

When I went through my wardrobe doing this level of clean out the underwear was the biggest thing that I noticed that didn't bring me Joy. I had some funky patterned ones that I had got as gifts over the years but other than that mine were all black boxer briefs. Usually, matching sets of three or four depending on the package they came in. I committed to over time changing out all of my underwear for ones that bring me Joy. Now my undies drawer is the 'fundies' drawer with a myriad of colours and prints. Many make me laugh because of the prints. Now I actually enjoy choosing what funderwear I'll be wearing that day.

Tip 1: Be rational – don't rationalize.
The best advice I can give is "think about it all rationally in terms of how to get what YOU want out of an area of your life". No one has better answers for what's best for you than YOU! Think rationally but don't rationalize your way out of doing something that you know needs to be done. Two VERY different things!

Tip 2: Context
When I went through this process and got to my sports clothes (I run, cycle, ski and do indoor rock climbing) I found it difficult to find clothes that were activity appropriate that brought me Joy. The activities certainly did but the clothes were more utilitarian than anything (like cycling shorts or running shoes or ski pants). I have a significant investment in these clothes, and it would really suck and be costly to replace all of these items with new ones. What I chose to do instead was to change my context around them so that they did bring me Joy. These items allowed me to do the things I love, they allowed me the access to do these things at the level that I enjoy doing them. When I put these items on, I look at it like I'm suiting up for Joy. Now even when I just look at these items I jump right to the Joy of that activity. I couldn't think of a different piece of clothing or equipment that would bring me more Joy from what I do.

As you can see it boils down to the context you have around an item. Anything can be associated with Joy just as anything can be associated with unhappiness. The trick is to be true and honest to your Self on what an item naturally holds for you. Don't hold on to something because you have an intention of one day changing your context around it because grandma gave it to you when you were four. I brought up the idea of context because sometimes it just takes a small shift in context to make something great in your life. If it takes a large amount of time and effort to change your context, then you're barking up the wrong tree and need to let it go. The more you can be honest with your Self, the greater your end result.

Tip 3: Being Complete
When you begin this process of letting things go it is of the utmost importance that you do so from a place of Love and Gratitude. What that looks like is for everything that you are removing from your life be grateful for it being there in the first place. It has served you well to create the awesome person that you are but now it's time for it to go to someone else to be part of their awesomeness. If you let go of something in your life that you are doing because you feel forced to or still have a connection to then you're not able to completely let it go energetically (you will have a negative attachment to it when you think about it). The most interesting thing about releasing things in gratitude is that it makes energetic space for new, bigger, better things to come into your life because you are filled with old connections that no longer serve you. Great side benefit!

MY OUTERMOST ENVIRONMENT

Person, Place, Thing, Event	Does NOT Bring Me Joy	Definitely Brings Me Joy	Could Bring Me Joy

Five things that I can do to make a difference in this environment in the next week.

	Task	Date to be Completed By
1.		
2.		
3.		
4.		
5.		

NOTES

_____

_____

_____

_____

_____

_____

_____

_____

_____

_____

_____

_____

_____

_____

MY INTERMEDIATE ENVIRONMENT

Person, Place, Thing, Event	Does NOT Bring Me Joy	Definitely Brings Me Joy	Could Bring Me Joy

Five things that I can do to make a difference in this environment in the next week.

	Task	Date to be Completed By
1.		
2.		
3.		
4.		
5.		

NOTES

_____

_____

_____

_____

_____

_____

_____

_____

_____

_____

_____

_____

_____

MY IMMEDIATE ENVIRONMENT

Person, Place, Thing, Event	Does NOT Bring Me Joy	Definitely Brings Me Joy	Could Bring Me Joy

Five things that I can do to make a difference in this environment in the next week.

	Task	Date to be Completed By
1.		
2.		
3.		
4.		
5.		

NOTES

_____

_____

_____

_____

_____

_____

_____

_____

_____

_____

_____

_____

_____

MY INTERNAL ENVIRONMENT

Person, Place, Thing, Event	Does NOT Bring Me Joy	Definitely Brings Me Joy	Could Bring Me Joy

Five things that I can do to make a difference in this environment in the next week.

	Task	Date to be Completed By
1.		
2.		
3.		
4.		
5.		

NOTES

_____

_____

_____

_____

_____

_____

_____

_____

_____

_____

_____

_____

_____

Some helpful questions for your internal environment

Emotional – Do you feel connected to your feelings and express them appropriately? Are you comfortable with the full range of emotions from love and joy to fear and anger? Are you comfortable with who you are being in your relationships? Are you happy with how you express yourself in all of your relationships?

Physical – How do you feel about your body? Are you comfortable in it? Do you like it? Are you physically active? Is your body healthy? Do you enjoy your sexuality? Are you a practical down to earth person? Are you highly independent and financially responsible? Are you comfortable in the material world?

Spiritual – Do you feel a sense of connection with a spiritual source? Are you connected to your intuitive guidance or inner wisdom? Do you ever feel a oneness with anything and everything? Do you spend or feel the need to spend time alone just 'being' or meditating?

Mental – Do you think and express yourself clearly? Are you highly impressionable when you are presented with new ideas? Are you open to new ideas? Do you believe you are fully self-expressed? Do you have a belief system that supports all aspects of You?

Three ideas that I've talked about over and over in this document are opportunity, being purposeful and being proactive. These are the keys to the castle.

It is important to look at this transition as an opportunity to create something brand new for yourself. Though a period of mourning the old you is very important in order to complete that chapter of your life, spending too much time fixated on your past can be of detriment to many aspects of the new life you're creating. The more you can see retirement as an opportunity the more you are freed up to get excited about what is to come and what you want to create.

Being purposeful and proactive as you move forward is the key to creating the life you want. Don't just fall through the next 40 to 60 years of your life and allow it to happen to you. Take this opportunity and give yourself some time to self-reflect, think about your needs and wants, then plan the direction you want to go. While it's true that life doesn't stand still, do what you need to be somewhat comfortable (i.e., making sure you have a roof over your head and you have money to use to eat) in the interim while you do this work. When you create your vision for the next chapter of your life, then approach it with the same focus and drive that you used to compete in sports.

Lastly, seek support in your retirement transition. As you know, it is not an easy thing to go through. In an interview with ESPN, former NFL running back Tiki Barber said this about his retirement transition: *"I couldn't figure out what to do next. It was strange to not have people telling me what to do because that was all I'd ever known. All of a sudden there was a malaise taking over me. I imagine that happens to a lot of players unless they're able to catch on to something."*

It is time to create your ow' team of professionals and loved"nes to help you move forward. Look at it this way, you've worked with a team of people to get you to the top of your game. Why wouldn't you work with someone or a team to help make this next chapter even better than the last?

> *"Our deepest fear is not that we are inadequate. Our deepest fear is that we are powerful beyond measure. It is our light, not our darkness that most frightens us. We ask ourselves, who am I to be brilliant, gorgeous, talented, fabulous? Actually, who are you not to be?"*
>
> **~ Marianne Williamson**

ACKNOWLEDGEMENTS

Beth Ostrander for helping me raise parts of this book to a level I certainly couldn't have by myself. The perfect person at the perfect time.

My Mother for all the encouragement and support no matter what and for editing everything I've ever written.

My amazing wife who is the absolute rock of my life. Having you as my anchor has allowed me to be a kite and find myself through blowing around in the chaotic breeze of life.

Thank you to the athletes who shared their stories so willingly to help others. Your stories have added so much colour to this book and I know your stories will help so many others.

MEET THE AUTHOR

S tuart's big word is "overcoming." Guiding people to overcome mental, emotional, and physical challenges is what feeds his soul. He has dedicated over twenty years educating others and has spent the last six years as an intuitive life and performance coach. Stuart is obsessed with why people do what they do and how small changes directly impact performance in all areas of life. He loves helping people find themselves through sports and play. He teaches others that "you can discover your true Self through sports. You just need to know where to look".

Stuart believes that the unique mindset and drive of professional athletes is a greatly untapped power that can change the world. As a transition coach for professional athletes entering retirement, Stuart helps athletes navigate this difficult time with efficiency and joy.

It typically takes people four to eight years to fully transition to a new chapter in life—Stuart helps you do it in one to two years. His objective is to take a period of upset and uncertainty and turn it into the most amazing time of your life. By doing this you build a new foundation in a way that will have the next chapter of your life be more fulfilling than your sports career.